THE JOURNEY OF *Faith*

BOBBY W. NORMAN

THE JOURNEY OF *Faith*

HOW TO HANG ON WHEN YOU'RE HURTING

AMBASSADOR INTERNATIONAL
GREENVILLE, SOUTH CAROLINA & BELFAST, NORTHERN IRELAND
www.ambassador-international.com

The Journey of Faith
How to Hang on When You're Hurting
©2024 by Bobby W. Norman
All rights reserved

ISBN: 978-1-64960-408-8, paperback
eISBN: 978-1-64960-456-9

Cover Design by Karen Slayne
Interior Typesetting by Dentelle Design
Edited by Katie Cruice Smith and Megan Griffin

No part of this publication may be reproduced, distributed, or transmitted in any form or by any means, including photocopying, recording, or other electronic or mechanical methods, without the prior written permission of the publisher, except in the case of brief quotations embodied in critical reviews and certain other noncommercial uses permitted by copyright law. For permission requests, contact the publisher using the information below.

Scripture taken from the King James Version of the Bible. Public Domain.

Ambassador International titles may be purchased in bulk for education, business, fundraising, or sales promotional use. For information, please email sales@emeraldhouse.com.

AMBASSADOR INTERNATIONAL
Emerald House
411 University Ridge, Suite B14
Greenville, SC 29601
United States
www.ambassador-international.com

AMBASSADOR BOOKS
The Mount
2 Woodstock Link
Belfast, BT6 8DD
Northern Ireland, United Kingdom
www.ambassadormedia.co.uk

The colophon is a trademark of Ambassador, a Christian publishing company.

This book is dedicated to

my wife Barbara Bauguess Norman.

You have been my companion for over fifty-two years.

I am forever grateful for your love and devotion.

The journey has not always been without rocky places;

but through it all, our faith has blazed a trail

for our children and grandchildren.

There is no one else I would rather have by my side!

I love you!

Contents

Preface 11
Author's Note 13
Introduction 15

Chapter One
Disaster 25

Chapter Two
Domestic Problems 31

Chapter Three
Job Explains His Pain 37

Chapter Four
You Are a Hypocrite 41

Chapter Five
I Am Not a Hypocrite 45

Chapter Six
You Deserve Punishment 47

Chapter Seven
God Is My Judge   51

Chapter Eight
You Are Lying   55

Chapter Nine
I Am Speaking Truth   59

Chapter Ten
You Are Evil   65

Chapter Eleven
You Are Miserable Comforters   69

Chapter Twelve
You Are Going to Hell   73

Chapter Thirteen
I Have a Redeemer!   77

Chapter Fourteen
You Have Robbed the Poor   83

Chapter Fifteen
The Wicked Are Allowed to Prosper   87

Chapter Sixteen
You Mistreat Orphans   89

Chapter Seventeen
Job Succumbs to Grief   93

Chapter Eighteen
You Can Never Be Clean — 99

Chapter Nineteen
God Is Known through Nature — 101

Chapter Twenty
Job Proclaims His Innocence — 105

Chapter Twenty-one
Job Continues His Lesson About God — 107

Chapter Twenty-two
Job Reminisces About the Past — 109

Chapter Twenty-three
Job Takes Steps in Guaranteed Holiness — 113

Chapter Twenty-four
Elihu Speaks — 117

Chapter Twenty-five
Job, You Are Wrong — 125

Chapter Twenty-six
I Have Perfect Knowledge — 129

Chapter Twenty-seven
God's Questions — 133

Chapter Twenty-eight
Job Confesses His Ignorance — 141

Chapter Twenty-nine
God Reveals His Power 143

Chapter Thirty
Job Worships 149

Chapter Thirty-one
God Rebukes Job's Friends 155

Epilogue
God Restores Job 161

A Word of Encouragement 167
Acknowledgments 171
About the Author 173

Preface

The *Journey of Faith* is an exposition of the Old Testament book of Job. The story concerns a very wealthy man, who suffers a complete reversal of his fortunes: his farm and caravan animals are stolen; his crops are destroyed; and his ten children are killed. Job's wife wishes he would die, and his three friends accuse him of sinning against God as evidenced by his loss.

In the face of all these oppositions, Job holds fast to his faith in God. Sometimes, that faith causes him to soar to the mountaintop of revelation, where he looks into the very face of God with complete assurance that everything is going to turn out all right. Sometimes, his faith virtually carries him through the dark valley of doubt, confusion, and depression. Over and over, his three friends debate their point that godly people always prosper while wicked people are always punished for their sins. Since Job is suffering, he is undoubtedly a wicked man.

But Job's faith prevails! Faith holds on to God until God chooses to reveal Himself—at which point, nothing else matters. When God shows up, everything else seems superficial and petty. God does not answer a single question that Job asked; but when He arrives on the scene, the questions are unimportant.

The Journey of Faith is the chronicle of one man's faith, which sustains him for the duration of his trials, and it is a ray of hope for those in times of personal crisis. If faith in God worked for Job, it will work for us, too!

Author's Note

The journey of faith can begin anywhere. Where there is a seed of hope planted in a heart that has been pierced by the anointed Word of God, faith can sprout. It has happened in a prison cell as a hardened criminal hears the story of the One Who came to set captives free. It has happened in a hospital room when the news was not good, but the spirit refused to break. It has happened in the funeral parlor as the one left weeping decides not to say goodbye but to honor their loved one by being faithful to God. It has happened at the birth of a child as parents realize that the best thing they can offer is an example. Faith has taken root in churches, homes, and schools—indeed, anywhere there is a person who can look from their lack to God's abundance. For that is what faith is, simply trusting God to do what He said He would do in the good times and the bad.

My wife, Barbara, began her journey of faith at a slumber party at a friend's house. For our oldest daughter, Jennifer, it began in a Vacation Bible School class at the age of seven. Our middle daughter, Heather, asked to be baptized when she was eight years old. I explained that to be baptized, you must first be saved. She wanted to know how you did that. I then explained that you must believe that Jesus is the Son of God and that He died for us on the cross, and then you invite Him into your heart to be your Savior.

"Well, Daddy, I've done all that!" she said with a tone of voice that made me wonder how I could have ever had any questions.

We took our eight-year-old daughter to the river to bury her old nature in water baptism, according to the commandment of our Lord. When did it start for her? I do not know, and neither does she; but somehow, in the soft, fertile soil of a child's heart, the seed of faith took root and started growing. It has the promise of becoming a strong, vibrant faith that she can pass along to others.

Our youngest daughter, Brittany, went to the altar at five years old and confessed Jesus as her Savior. That Sunday afternoon, her mom heard her on her swing singing joyfully. Even at that young age, she had found the joy of salvation. She has matured into a wonderful, caring wife and mother, passing her faith on to another generation.

My own journey of faith began at an altar in the church my family attended. I was eleven years old. A duet from Tennessee, Don and Earl, were singing when I felt the hand of the gentle Galilean and heard the invitation from the Royal Family to become a child of God. As I knelt in that altar, I knew beyond any shadow of a doubt that my sins were forgiven and that my name was added to the family register in Heaven. Since then, I have had the time of my life!

The book of Job is the account of one man's journey of faith. It is an intensely emotional journey—one minute in the lowest pit of depression and despair, the next on the highest peak of revelation and joy. But through it all, faith held Job securely until he looked into the face of God. That is what faith does—it gives us the vision to see with our heart, even when our eyes are blind. As we follow Job's story, we will feel our own faith stretching, maturing, and becoming strong enough for whatever we face on our journey.

—*Bobby Norman*

Introduction

Let me introduce you to the book of Job with a little quiz.

1. Are you experiencing any sickness or disease?
2. Are you suffering any pain or sorrow?
3. Are you behind in paying your bills?
4. Do you have to wonder each month where the money is coming from to cover your expenses?

Now, let Job's three friends grade the quiz for you. If you answered yes to any of these questions, you are a hypocrite! You go to church, sing, pray, and testify like a true believer. You say that you love God; but your sickness, pain, and suffering prove that you are a backslider and that God no longer recognizes you as His child. If you are going through any financial difficulty, you are simply not saved. You try to look righteous; but God, Who knows your heart, is punishing you for your wickedness. If you would repent of your sins and turn from your iniquity, God would heal all your sickness, erase all your suffering, pay all your bills, and cause you to live in super-abundance. If you were a Christian, you would not have problems!

How do you feel right now about these statements? I want you to remember that feeling because that is the way Job feels for most of this book as his three friends try to convince him that abundance equals righteousness and that suffering means that you have sinned. If you will remember the anger, confusion, and hurt you are feeling now, you will understand Job a little better. You will be able to better identify with him as he faces the greatest trial of his faith at the hands of his three friends.

Background

The book of Job is categorized as a book of poetry, along with Psalms, Proverbs, Ecclesiastes, Song of Solomon, and Lamentations. Hebrew poetry is expressed by the repetition of ideas, rather than by rhyme or meter. All the conversation in the book of Job is in poetic form.

The book of Job is also considered part of the wisdom literature of the Bible because it is drawn from the experiences of life and teaches us about the meaning of life. In particular, it teaches about suffering and faith in God, even in trying times.

Job is probably the oldest book in the Bible, written in an older version of Hebrew. Tradition tells us that it was written by Moses while he was tending his father-in-law's sheep in the Midian desert. From there, it was delivered to the Hebrew slaves in Egypt to encourage them during their time of suffering, giving them hope of deliverance. It takes place before the institution of the priesthood because Job offers up sacrifices for his family instead of taking the animal to a priest to be slaughtered. The Law expressly forbade any offerings for sin except those done by the priests.

Another reason for believing that Job is a very old manuscript is the length of Job's life. He lived to be 240 years old, which puts him in the class of the patriarchs like Abraham, Isaac, and Jacob. As history progressed, men lived much shorter lives.

In addition to Moses, there are two other possible authors: Job himself or Elihu, who appears in the debate in chapter thirty-two. The narrative of Elihu's speech is told in the first-person singular, which could indicate authorship (i.e., "I said."). At any rate, we who believe in the inspiration of Scripture know that God is the ultimate Author of all His Word; and we accept the accuracy of the message even when we do not know the identity of the messenger.

The theme of the book of Job is the development of faith. During one of his mountaintop revelations during his persecution, Job makes a startling declaration of faith. He says, "Though [God] slay me, yet will I trust in him" (13:15). Job teaches us that we can have confidence in God, even during our suffering and affliction. In our pain and grief, we can look to the God of creation and find strength and comfort. If we keep looking to God during those times of trouble, He will lead us to a revelation of Himself.

Job declares in the last chapter, "I have heard of thee by the hearing of the ear: but now mine eye seeth thee" (42:5). It is one thing to know *about* God; it is quite another to *see* God. But the whole story assures us that if we keep looking to God during our time of testing and heartache, God will show up. Faith keeps its eye on God instead of on the problems.

Job: The Man

Job 1:1–3

Allow me to introduce you to Job by giving you a list of the characteristics ascribed to him in chapter one.

His name means "one who is hated." God holds the man in very high regard—as we will see later—so Satan must be the one who hates Job. Satan is the enemy of all who believe in God, and we never expect to be on friendly terms with him. Any person who attempts to live a life of faith in God can expect to encounter opposition. But be of good cheer—the power of God is greater than the power of Satan. To be loved of God and hated by Satan is a good combination!

Job was a very patient man. "Behold, we count them happy which endure. Ye have heard of the patience of Job" (James 5:11). Few could have endured the physical suffering, personal loss, the attack on his faith, and the insults of his friends as Job did. Truly, Job's patience indicates a remarkable faith in God.

Job was a man of character. Toward his fellow man, Job was perfect and upright. He treated others with respect and courtesy, honoring them as children of God, in no way belittling or harming them. His love for people was a powerful display of his love for God. Toward God, Job was reverent. He feared God, which is "the beginning of wisdom" (Prov. 9:10).

Ezekiel 14:14 refers to Job as one of the three most righteous men on record (Noah and Daniel being the other two). Job stood in awe at the power of a holy and righteous God. Not only was Job a man of character toward others and toward God, but he was also a man of character toward himself. He avoided evil. Nothing reveals a man's character more than what he allows when no one is watching. Job was a man of character in the presence of his friends, and he was still a man of high moral character when he was alone. When no one is looking, what movies do you watch, or what magazines do you read? That is a reflection of our character!

Job was a loving father. He had seven sons and three daughters, and he was very concerned about their welfare. In our story, they are already grown with homes of their own, but he never ceases to express his concern for their welfare.

Job was a wealthy man. His list of assets includes seven thousand sheep, three thousand camels, five hundred yoke of oxen, five hundred female donkeys, a nice home, pastureland for all his livestock, and a multitude of servants to look after his affairs. Job was such a wealthy man that he was considered "the greatest of all the men of the east" (1:3). Typical of his age (and ours), greatness was measured by money not character.

Most importantly, Job was a praying man. He continually offered sacrifice to God as intercession for his children. As was common before the giving of the Law, Job served as the priest for his family. Throughout the book, we see Job carrying on conversations with God. We maintain a vibrant faith only by frequent communication with the Father.

Job is a picture of Christ and the suffering He endured for us. We can say of him, as it was said of Jesus, "It pleased the LORD to bruise him" (Isa. 53:10).

Just as Abraham's offering of Isaac pointed to the crucifixion of Jesus, the suffering of Job points to the One Who would come to suffer for the sins of the whole world.

The book of Job contains teachings which have become foundational to our Christian doctrine: intercessory prayer, Satan's access to Heaven, Satan as the accuser of the saints, and Satan's limitations. Several of these themes are discussed nowhere else in the Bible. Our understanding of God would be poorer without the Book of Job.

Intercessory Prayer
Job 1:4–5

Job was a father who believed in praying for his children individually and continually. He prayed for them by name, "according to the number of them all." Every parent should call each of his children's names before the Father on a daily basis. God, as a Father, honors our prayers of intercession for our children.

I started praying for my children individually many years ago. I pray for their spiritual development, their education, their careers, their health, and their spouses. Through the years, I have come to believe that the welfare of my children, now and in the future, rests in the hands of a loving God Whom I have learned to trust with the things most precious to me in this world. What a great peace of mind I have from entrusting my children to a Father Who loves them even more than I do. What a relief from worry to know that God has all things planned for their future. Now that my three girls are married, I tease their husbands that if I had known what God was sending, I would have prayed harder! But God has truly given me three great sons-in-law who have blessed me with seven grandchildren. Intercessory prayer works!

Job did not have the power to absolve the sins of his children through his sacrifices any more than any other person has the power to forgive sins, but he knew that God greatly honors intercessory prayers from His children on behalf of others. When God will not answer selfish prayers, He sometimes answers sel*fless* prayers. Lot was rescued from Sodom because Abraham prayed (Gen. 19:29). Paul prayed daily for all the churches under his care (Col. 1:3) We have a great opportunity afforded to us through the power of prayer.

Satan's Access to Heaven:
Job 1:6-7

It seems offensive for Satan to have access to Heaven after God kicked him out because of his rebellion (Isa. 14:12). It seems that he should not be allowed anywhere near the holy throne room of God. But the book of Job teaches us some powerful truths about the one we call the devil.

First of all, his habitation is planet Earth. Satan came into the presence of God "from going to and fro in the earth, and from walking up and down in it" (v. 7). Second Corinthians 4:4 calls him "the god of this world." Ephesians 2:2 says he is "the prince of the power of the air, the spirit that now worketh in the children of disobedience." The admonition of I Peter 5:8 says, "Be sober, be vigilant; because your adversary the devil, as a roaring lion, walketh about, seeking whom he may devour."

Notice the power of Satan corrupting the handiwork of God—murder, rape, lying, stealing, hatred, division, break-ups, and breakdowns. Surely, Satan has stamped his name on our planet, and his evil influence is all around us. Jesus called him "the thief" who comes only "to steal, and to kill, and to destroy" (John 10:10).

But Satan must still report to God. When all the created beings came to bring a report to the Creator, Satan had to report also. God has the authority to call him on the carpet and demand an accounting for his actions. Satan is not the great power of the universe as he would lead us to believe. God is still in control, and *all* things are subject to Him, including Satan.

Satan as the Accuser of the Brethren:
Job 1:8–12

This section of Job has some powerful things to say about God's children. For instance, God is proud of His children. Look at His question to Satan. He sounds like a proud Dad.

"Hast thou considered my servant Job?" God continues to brag, "There is none like him in the earth" (v. 8).

I carry pictures of my family in my billfold and set pictures of them on my desk. My wife, children, and grandchildren are the greatest in the world. If you do not believe it, just ask me! Perhaps I brag too much sometimes, but it is only natural to boast about those you love. God does!

Do you understand that God loves you? I wonder how often He brags about us in Heaven. Jesus said if we were not ashamed to confess Him, He would not be ashamed to confess us before the Father and the holy angels (Luke 9:26). God loves to brag on His children, telling the angels how wonderful we are. God is proud to claim us as His own.

Satan is the accuser of the brethren. With God's words of praise still ringing in our ears, Satan begins his accusations. He brings up all our past sins and failures, and we must hang our heads in shame because his accusations are not false. There are an abundance of charges he can dig up to embarrass and humiliate the best of us.

But just when we are about to resign in disgrace, God whispers in our ears, "I turned in my book of records for that year, day, and hour; but that page is blank. There is no record in Heaven that you ever committed that sin. Your guilt has been thoroughly purged by the blood of Jesus. Child, hold up your head and continue on with your life. You are no longer guilty!"

Satan began to accuse Job of serving God only for the benefits involved. He asserted that if the benefits were taken away, Job would surely curse God. I have often wondered why God accepted Satan's challenge. Certainly, God knows all things, and He knew that Job would be true. Perhaps it was to prove to Satan that good is more powerful than evil. Perhaps it was for Job's benefit to see how much he could endure and how real his faith really was. Or perhaps it was for our benefit, to show us the power of faith in the midst of our problems. If Job could hold on to God through his troubles, surely I can stand the "light afflictions" I face (II Cor. 4:17).

There are great benefits to serving God. As believers, we have the greatest benefit package ever offered. Satan admitted that God has placed a hedge about us, our house, and all our possessions on every side. What a glorious security system God has provided for His family! The following are passages that show God's protection:

- "The angel of the Lord encampeth round about them that fear him, and delivereth them" (Psalm 34:7).
- "He that dwelleth in the secret place of the most High shall abide under the shadow of the Almighty. I will say of the LORD, He is my refuge and my fortress: my God; in him will I trust" (Psalm 91:1-2).
- "Ye are of God, little children, and have overcome them: because greater is he that is in you, than he that is in the world" (1 John 4:4).

Then Satan admitted that God has blessed our work. "Thou hast blessed the work of his hands" (Job 1:10). God decreed in the beginning that man would work six days out of seven. God has decreed that the work of our hands will provide bread for our table! Your occupation should bring glory and honor to God. Whatever you do for a living, allow the hand of God to bless it and make it a blessing to others.

Satan also admitted that God increases our substance or the things we own. "His substance is increased in the land" (Job 1:10). God never promised to make us rich, but He has promised to "supply all [we] need" (Phil. 4:19). Sow some seeds, and God will grant a blessed harvest. We see this time and again in Scripture:

- "Blessed be the Lord, who daily loadeth us with benefits" (Psalm 68:19).
- "Bless the LORD, O my soul: and all that is within me, bless his holy name. Bless the LORD, O my soul, and forget not all his benefits: Who forgiveth all thine iniquities; who healeth all thy diseases; Who redeemeth thy life from destruction; who crowneth thee with lovingkindness and tender mercies; Who satisfieth thy mouth with good things; so that thy youth is renewed like the eagle's" (Psalm 103:1-5).

Satan cannot touch a child of God without God's permission. Our "adversary" is "seeking whom he *may* devour" (I Peter 5:8, emphasis mine). The word *may* implies permission. God has set up a hedge that Satan cannot penetrate unless God allows it. Whatever we are going through has already been approved by our loving Father for some purpose in our lives. "And we know that all things work together for good to them that love God, to them who are the called according to his purpose" (Rom. 8:28).

God promises that He will not assign us a task too hard to bear. "There hath no temptation taken you but such as is common to man: but God is faithful, who will not suffer you to be tempted above that ye are able; but will with the temptation also make a way to escape, that ye may be able to bear it" (I Cor. 10:13).

God sets limits on Satan's influence. God sets very specific guidelines on Satan's activity. Satan was allowed to take all of Job's possessions but not to touch Job himself. I don't know what you are going through, but God knows; and He will let Satan go only so far before He says it is enough.

We are about to see that play out in Job's life as he is met with one disaster after another. Job does not know what has been going on in the heavenly realm—that God has given Satan permission to attack his earthly possessions. But Job will be held accountable for how he responds, just as we all are responsible for how we respond to trials.

CHAPTER ONE
Disaster

JOB'S ACCOUNT
JOB 1:13-19

My seven sons and three daughters were having another of their weekly feasts at my oldest son's house. Oh, how I pray they are not sinning in their partying! I pray for them every day to follow after God. But at least, they are all getting along and celebrating together! I offer sacrifices on their behalf to cover their reveling.

I was thinking about my family when I saw a messenger running toward me with news that I already sensed would be bad. Breathlessly, he reported, "The oxen were plowing, and the asses feeding beside them. And the Sabeans fell upon them and took them away; yea, they have slain the servants with the edge of the sword; and I only am escaped alone to tell thee" (Job 1:14-15).

I was stunned. Five hundred yoke of oxen had plowed my fields and harvested my crops for many, many years. With them gone, I would have to find some other way to get the plowing and harvesting done. Think of the replacement cost for one thousand oxen! My income for the year was looking bleak.

But another messenger was already giving his report. "The fire of God is fallen from heaven, and hath burned up the sheep, and the servants, and consumed them: and I only am escaped alone to tell thee" (Job 1:16).

All my oxen are gone, and now all my sheep? Fire came from Heaven? Am I dreaming? I am staggered at the news! The wool mills and the butcher shops will be at a loss for a while. No other shepherd will be able to supply the volume I was supplying. People in the village will go hungry without my mutton and naked without my wool. I was trying to sort out in my mind why all this was happening to me, but someone interrupted my thoughts.

"The Chaldeans made out three bands, and fell upon the camels, and have carried them away, yea, and slain the servants with the edge of the sword; and I only am escaped alone to tell thee" (Job 1:17).

The camels are taken, too? Three thousand caravan camels are gone, stolen by Chaldeans. How will I transport my merchandise to and from the far corners of the earth? How can my business survive such a loss?

I had little time to contemplate these business matters because another messenger was coming. I could tell that his news was devastating.

"Thy sons and thy daughters were eating and drinking wine in their eldest brother's house: And, behold, there came a great wind from the wilderness, and smote the four corners of the house, and it fell upon the young men, and they are dead; and I only am escaped alone to tell thee" (Job 1:18-19). My mind struggled to comprehend the incomprehensible news.

It's not the season for the dreaded whirlwinds from the south. My beautiful girls! My strong sons! All are gone? Crushed under the house? Dead? Not my precious babies! Thoughts churned through my tormented mind until I had to do something. Like my forefathers in times of severe stress, I ripped my robe in two and threw it on the ground. I ran into the house for my razor to shave my head. I tried these normal forms of expressing grief which have been practiced since the beginning of time. I had to give vent to my anguish lest I die under the load of sorrow. I needed to let everyone know the sorrow of my heart and the dark anguish of my soul. I cried out to God, "Oh, God, how it hurts. Oh, God, I can't stand it. Oh, God."

God! That's it—God! Only God can sustain me. Only He can keep me from going crazy with grief and despair. There in the yard, I fell on the ground before the God of all creation. In my anguish, I began to worship Him and thank Him for all His past blessings—for the times He met with me in my prayer time, for His strength down through the years, for all the good times I have enjoyed.

As I remembered how good God had been to me, the only thing I could do was to praise Him. I came into this world with nothing, and I will leave with nothing; but for a while, God loaned me more than I deserved. If God now wants back what He loaned me, that is His business. If I have accepted good at the hand of God, I should be prepared to accept the bad also. Blessed is Your name, O Lord. I love You and worship You. You are altogether lovely.

Commentary

Job 1:20–2:8

I have never seen such faith! Job had just lost everything he owned, including his dear children. Yet in his grief, he worshipped God. He did not sin with his lips but used them to lift up praise to the Lord. Most people going through such a time of suffering would curse their luck, blaming God for their trouble. Most people would question, "Why me? What did I ever do to God to deserve this?" But as Job reminds us, none of us deserve even the least of God's blessings. If we got what we deserved, we would be in Hell! Job found comfort in releasing everything he had back to the hands of God—not an easy process and certainly not an immediate process. Job went through a time of grieving before he reached the point of surrender.

During his time of grief, Job did not sin with his lips by blaming God. He found strength to go on living through worship. Even though he did not understand what was happening to him, his faith found refuge in the arms of a mighty God.

What a great lesson this is for us! We can collapse in a fit of rage and spend the rest of our life cursing God, or we can simply lean heavily on Him and let Him bear the load. His shoulders are bigger than ours, and His back is strong enough to bear any load. We can "[cast] all [our cares] upon him; for he careth for [us]" (I Peter 5:7).

Satan was wrong. Job passed Satan's test with flying colors. But Satan is nothing if not persistent. He came back into the ring for the second round, primed for a victory. Job might win one battle, but we will see what he does the next time around.

Here is another important lesson for believers. Never rest on your laurels over some victory you have won. The minute you drop your guard and get careless is when Satan will come with a new tactic to defeat you. It was after Elijah won the contest on Mount Carmel that he was most susceptible to Jezebel's threats (I Kings 18). Maintain your vigilance, "looking unto Jesus the author and finisher of our faith" (Heb. 12:2).

Back to the book of Job, we see that once again, Satan is forced to present himself to God, listening in fury as God again brags on Job. "There is none like him in the earth, a perfect and an upright man, one that feareth God, and escheweth evil" (Job 2:3). God repeated the list from their previous encounter, then added a new boast: "and still he holdeth fast his integrity, although thou movedst me against him, to destroy him without cause" (Job 2:3).

God is basically saying to Satan, "You wanted Me to test him by taking away all his material blessings, and I did. But Job passed the test! He still stands! He still maintains his integrity! He still loves Me, despite his losses. Satan, Job won!"

God is so pleased when His children walk in faith. He devotes forty verses in Hebrews 11 to the Faith Hall of Fame—just bragging on His children for their consistent faith.

But Satan makes another bid for Job. He counters that all men have their price. Everyone has a weak spot somewhere. So, Satan challenges God that if

He will touch Job's body, he will curse God. Men value their health more than their wealth, right?

Unfortunately, Satan is right about a lot of people. Esau's price for compromise was a bowl of stew to ease his hunger. Achan sold out for a wedge of gold, some silver, and a Babylonian garment—possessions which were worthless in a barren desert. Judas went to Hell over thirty pieces of silver. May God help us to be faithful, regardless of the cost, to never sell out to Satan for momentary pleasures or give up our faith for cheap thrills. God, give us faith that will stand the test!

Again, Satan could accuse but not move against Job without permission. Sometimes, we ourselves give Satan permission to come against us by our lack of faith in God or by our confessions of doubt and unbelief. Sometimes, God gives Satan permission to carry out a certain plan for purposes known only to Him. But remember, God always sets limits on Satan's activities. God allowed Satan to touch Job's body but not his life. He could afflict him physically but not kill him.

Determined to win Job, Satan chose boils as his weapon. It was a great choice for maximum pain. Look at Job sitting on the ash heap covered in boils from head to toe. Notice those running, festering sores, which itch so badly Job must scratch them continually with a broken piece of pottery. Sitting on the ash heap, he is all alone. There is not a friend in sight. Where are his wife, his physician, his few faithful servants who escaped the catastrophes, his closest companions? None appear as he sits alone scraping his boils and rubbing ashes on his sores, wincing in agony with each stroke of the pottery shard.

Ashes are good medicine, easing the itch or slowing the spread of sores. But from time immemorial, the ash heap has been a symbol of repentance. Jesus said of the cities of Chorazin and Bethsaida, "If the mighty works, which were done in you, had been done in Tyre and Sidon, they would have repented long ago in sackcloth and ashes" (Matt. 11:21). Daniel also sat in sackcloth and ashes while he prayed to God (Dan. 9:3).

In the book of Esther, ashes are a symbol of mourning.

> When Mordecai perceived all that was done, Mordecai rent his clothes, and put on sackcloth with ashes, and went out into the midst of the city, and cried with a loud and a bitter cry; And came even before the king's gate: for none might enter into the king's gate clothed with sackcloth. And in every province, whithersoever the king's commandment and his decree came, there was great mourning among the Jews, and fasting, and weeping, and wailing; and many lay in sackcloth and ashes" (Esther 4:1-3).

Whether Job's reason was for medicine, repentance, mourning, or prayer, it is certainly evident that he had humbled himself before God and submitted everything to His will. He had gone down as far as possible. He had no sheep left with which to offer sacrifice, no money left with which to purchase an offering, no place of position or authority left to submit to God. So Job offers the only thing he has left—himself. Maybe in the long run, that is all God wants.

CHAPTER TWO
Domestic Problems

JOB'S ACCOUNT
JOB 2:8-10

As I sit alone on the ash heap, I pray for my grieving wife who has not spoken to me since we buried our children. She brings food occasionally to keep me from starving, barely acknowledging my presence. Her shoulders are weighed down with unbearable grief, her eyes swollen from crying, her hair and clothing in disarray. She looks like a corpse, wandering between the homes of our children as if waiting for their return.

When she finally speaks, her words pierce my heart like a sword. "Do you still think you are Mr. Perfect? You call yourself a believer, offering sacrifices each day for our children, parading through town like a self-righteous celebrity. Now look at you. Is your righteousness any benefit to you now? Where is your God now? He has failed you. Why don't you give up your worthless faith? Why don't you kill yourself and get out of my sight? Perhaps if you cursed your God, He would kill you Himself. At least you would be out of your misery instead of sitting here like a mangy beast."

As she walks away, I try to explain how blessed we are. God has blessed us with everything our hearts could desire. For many years, we have experienced the goodness that only comes from serving God. How can we turn our backs on Him now?

"Dear wife," I plead, "your sorrow has caused you to speak foolishly. Is it reasonable to accept the blessings of God and reject the trouble that life brings? Can we expect everything to be good all the time? It is faith in God that sustains me even at the lowest point in my life."

She doesn't even look back or acknowledge my words. I'm still sitting on the ash heap praying for my grieving wife.

Commentary

Just when it seems nothing else could possibly go wrong, Mrs. Job comes onto the scene with an attitude—nagging, blaming, screeching in Job's ears. Can a man who has maintained his faith stand up under the constant harping of a woman deprived of her children and her way of life?

Did Satan get permission from God to make Mrs. Job react this way? Had the loss of her children caused this great bitterness in her spirit? Had her fall from the elite society of the day spoiled her character? Was she always a negative harpy? Why did God take everything else Job had and leave a nagging wife? Did Satan have permission to take her, too, but left her just to torment Job further? These are questions without answers, but we can feel the added weight in Job's spirit as she comes fuming up the path to the ash heap to pour out her scorn on the husband of her youth.

Can't you just hear her now? "Don't tell me you're still alive. I wish God had killed you along with my children. They were more worthy of life than you. Are you still holding on to this God Who has allowed all this happen to us? Why would you even pray to a God like that anymore? You act like you still think you are a righteous man. Give up on all that nonsense. Go ahead and curse God, so you can die and get out of your misery. You are holding on to a faith that doesn't work and a God Who doesn't care. Give it up. Just looking at you reminds me of all I have lost."

One of the hardest trials to a person's faith is a spouse who doesn't share their faith or who deliberately tries to undermine their righteousness.

Nothing cuts worse than criticism from the one who is "bone of [your] bones, and flesh of [your] flesh" (Gen. 2:23). Watch Mrs. Job standing there with her hands on her hips, spouting poison, turning the air around her blue with her curses. Perhaps Jesus was thinking of her when he taught, "A man's foes shall be they of his own household" (Matt. 10:36). It is interesting that we know the names of his three daughters but not the name of his wife. Hopefully, God did not write her off. But don't spend too much time looking at her—rather look at Job and listen to his reaction. Nothing proves his faith more than his reaction to his nagging wife.

"But he said unto her, Thou speakest as one of the foolish women speaketh. What? shall we receive good at the hand of God, and shall we not receive evil?" (Job 2:10). Praise God for faith that hangs on!

Another example we see of this is found in Genesis 32. Jacob has been wrestling with the angel of the Lord all night. Toward morning, the angel asked Jacob to release him because daylight was breaking, but Jacob said, "I will not let thee go, except thou bless me" (Gen. 32:26). The angel changed Jacob's name to Israel for "as a prince hast thou power with God and with men, and hast prevailed" (Gen. 32:28). Jacob went from that place of wrestling with God to become the father of twelve sons who would form the twelve tribes of Israel. Even today, there is a nation named Israel in his honor because he hung on to God against all hope.

Shammah was one of the judges of Israel during a time of Philistine conquest. These "People of the Sea" plagued Israel by raiding their crops during every harvest. But Shammah had had enough! The historian recorded, "And the Philistines were gathered together into a troop, where was a piece of ground full of lentiles: and the people fled from the Philistines. But he stood in the midst of the ground, and defended it, and slew the Philistines: and the LORD wrought a great victory" (II Sam. 23:11-12). Sometimes, faith must get exasperated enough with the status quo to stand up and say, "That is enough. I'm not going to take any more!"

Pharaoh was trying to get Moses to compromise. He told Moses that he could go wherever he wanted to go but could not take his flocks and herds of animals. Moses, full of faith in God, looked Pharaoh in the eyes and said, "Our cattle also shall go with us; there shall not an hoof be left behind" (Exod. 10:26). And the One Who moves heaven and earth to keep His word, led the children of Israel out of Egyptian bondage with a mighty hand with every piece of livestock they owned. When you know the Word of God, stand firm, despite the forces that come against you—even a nagging spouse! Your faith will see you through.

Later in the story, we see Job confessing that he is going to live forever. He will not commit suicide; rather, he will commit everything to God and trust Him with all his heart.

A Friend Indeed
Job 2:11-13

Job's wife has been a disappointment in helping him to deal with his sorrow because her own sorrows were more than she could bear, but there is hope coming over the hill. Three of Job's friends have heard of his troubles and have joined forces to comfort him. You will hear some very negative things coming from these men later, so it is best to point out their good points first. Despite their later treatment of Job, they really are good friends at heart. They are not after his money—he has no money left. They are not after his assistance—he cannot even help himself. They only want to help their long-time friend.

They came to mourn with him and were successful. They came to comfort him and failed. But they are there. Even his wife has turned her back on Job, but these three are there in his darkest hour. Friends share the good times and the bad times equally.

Before they start debating, let me introduce these three friends. First, there is Eliphaz the Temanite. Teman was a grandson of Esau (Gen. 36:10-11), so it is reasonable to assume that Eliphaz was also a descendant of Esau. His name means "God is strength." It is too bad that Eliphaz relies on his own strength and wisdom during the debates instead of waiting for a true word from the Lord. Instead, he comes equipped with all the answers. He believes he is God's mouthpiece—there to set Job straight.

The second friend is Bildad the Shuhite. Shuah was a son of Abraham and his second wife Keturah (Gen. 25:2). The name Bildad means "son of contention." During the debates, he will be very cruel in his remarks to Job. He completely ignores Job's despair, telling him to look to the tradition of their forefathers for his answers. All the questions have been answered by the previous generations of wise men.

Finally, there is Zophar the Naamithite. Naamah is in northern Arabia, making Zophar an Arabian. His name means "departing early." Perhaps the implication is that he gives up on Job's friendship. He, too, is very cruel in his attack on Job. He is a legalist. You must do things in a certain way for God to respond. But if you follow the correct formula, God will react in the way He is supposed to. It seems they think they have God trained to act on their command. Say the magic words, and God will perform. How little Zophar knows of the true God.

Watch as these three friends come up the road to meet Job. They have made an appointment to comfort Job; but as they approach his home, they fail to recognize the man. His sores and his sorrows have altered his appearance beyond recognition. Instead of the self-confident businessman they know, here is a man who seems beaten down in defeat, covered from head to toe with oozing boils and pungent ashes. Job presents a pitiful picture.

Once they understand that this pitiful-looking creature is the man they seek, they lift their voices and weep, sincerely touched by his pain. A person can never effectively minister to someone else's suffering until God allows them to feel that suffering in their own spirit. Second Corinthians 1:4 says, "Who comforteth us in all our tribulation, that we may be able to comfort them which are in any trouble, by the comfort wherewith we ourselves are comforted of God." These men so identify with Job's pain and suffering that they tear their own clothes in imitation of him and sprinkle dust on their heads, just as Job had done in the traditional symbolism of mourning. They enter fully into his mourning.

Then, they sit down, stooping to get on his level. They get down in the ashes with him! It is one thing to stand over someone, pointing a finger at them and preaching a sermon. It is quite another thing to reach out in love and compassion, finding common ground where healing can begin. Sometimes (most times?), God will not use a sermon or a lecture but a hand of friendship. Oh, God, reach out to others through our hands.

So, here they sit on the ash heap with Job; and for seven days, they honor his extreme sorrow by their silence. When you are around people who are hurting, every minute does not need to be filled with sound. Be still and sit quietly. Sometimes, the best thing you can do is just be there lending silent support. Make sure the grieving person feels free to speak first. These three were very good friends as long as they were silent.

CHAPTER THREE
Job Explains His Pain

JOB'S ACCOUNT
JOB 3:1-26

My friends have been so patient with me, but I can't help it. I have to express how I feel!

"I wish I had never been born! I curse that day! I would have been better off if my mother was unable to conceive. I don't know why I was even born! She could have stopped my birth or refused to feed me after I was born. Many babies are born prematurely or fail to mature in the womb. Why did the midwife let me live? Why was I born to experience only misery and bitterness?

"I long for death now. I rejoice at the thought of death like one rejoicing over finding a treasure. But God has made me a prisoner to life. I cannot escape. I sigh in misery and roar in pain until I am weak as water. My worst fears have been realized. My greatest nightmare has come true. I was minding my own business when trouble invaded my life. Now, my life is over. I can't carry on like this!"

Commentary

Have you ever been depressed or felt like there was no reason to live? Disappointment comes when plans are disrupted. You are plagued with guilt because of failures in your life. You are hurt over a friend's unfaithfulness.

Everyone experiences those times; indeed, the Bible tells the story of many people who suffered from depression.

The prophet Jeremiah had been preaching to people who mocked him for so long that he became discouraged. "O LORD, thou hast deceived me, and I was deceived . . . I am in derision daily, every one mocketh me. For since I spake, I cried out, I cried violence and spoil; because the word of the LORD was made a reproach unto me, and a derision, daily. Then I said, I will not make mention of him, nor speak any more in his name" (Jer. 20:7-9). If preaching the Word was going to get him in so much trouble, he just would not do it anymore. If people were too stubborn to listen to the prophet of God, they could just go to torment!

Jeremiah quickly conquered his depression, for he goes on to say, "But his word was in mine heart as a burning fire shut up in my bones, and I was weary with forbearing, and I could not stay" (Jer. 20:9). Being the victim of a joke is hard to take. Being the odd man out takes a lot of grace. Many who have taken a stand for Christ against the culture of the day have found themselves ostracized, and that is a fertile breeding ground for depression. May God give us faith to stand on His Word, even if we must stand alone. May He give us grace to keep on telling the news, even when others make fun and reject the message.

Jonah is another prophet who became depressed. He was upset because God had mercy on Nineveh. He had tried to run away from the call of God because he wanted God to destroy the pagan city. If he preached to them, they would repent; and God would spare them. But they were the enemy and deserved to be wiped out! They were heathens who did not deserve God's mercy in Jonah's opinion.

God used a storm at sea and a reserved room in the belly of a whale to convince Jonah to obey. Everyone, including the king, repented; and just like Jonah had feared, God showed them mercy and spared their lives. So Jonah got angry.

"Therefore now, O LORD, take I beseech thee, my life from me; for it is better for me to die than to live" (Jonah 4:3). Jonah was thinking about his reputation back at home. His friends would never let him forget that Nineveh's survival was his fault. The opinion of men was more important than the salvation of souls and doing the will of God. Sometimes, we, too, are guilty of wanting fireworks instead of mercy on our enemies.

One of the greatest things you can do for someone who is depressed is to listen. Let them talk and get all those feelings out in the open. Depressed people will say stupid things in their passion, but allow them to express their feelings without criticism. Let them talk. If you start being judgmental, they will clam up and internalize all that garbage until it ruins their life. People need to talk through their problems, even when the words out of their mouth make no sense.

The second thing you can do is love them. Accept the depressed person just as they are. Sure, they need to mature. Sure, some of the things they say will border on heresy, but they need love and acceptance more than a lecture at this point. Let them know that you care for them, regardless of what they do or say. Give them enough genuine love to make them feel secure during this precarious time. You do not have to agree with their depression or their response to it—you just have to love the person.

Only after listening and loving can you lead. Lead them gently to the Word of God. Show them the promises. Explain the truth. Lead them to acceptance of what God said about their situation. Finally, lead them in prayer. Take their problems to God in faith and leave them in His hands. May the God of grace minister to you as you minister to those who are depressed.

Now, let's see how Job's friends handle the situation and whether they are the friends God has called them to be.

CHAPTER FOUR
You Are a Hypocrite

ELIPHAZ'S ACCOUNT
JOB 4:1–5:27

I, Eliphaz, need to say something. Job needs to be set straight. God would not want me to be silent!

"Job, would it grieve you too much if we tried to talk to you? I am going to tell you what I think regardless because you are a first-rate hypocrite! You counseled many people and gave hope to many who were ready to give up. You encouraged others and caused them to rise to action. You told everyone else how to cope with problems; but now that trouble has come upon you, you have fainted. Suffering has touched you, and you are depressed. Is this how you show your faith in God? Is this how God rewards righteousness? You cannot even follow your own advice. You are a failure!"

Job's face says it all, but I cannot be silent. I must continue!

"Think about it, Job! Do innocent people end up on the ash heap? Do righteous people face the wrath of God? Those who sow wickedness reap wickedness. God can take out the wicked with just one blast from His nostrils! He breaks the teeth of lions, so they perish for lack of prey. If God destroys evil men with His breath and punishes cruel animals, He must really be upset with you!

"Job, I know a secret! God revealed something to me in a scary dream. A spirit passed right in front of me, making my hair stand on end and my bones to shake. I could barely discern an outline of something before my eyes.

"Then in the silence, I heard a voice saying, 'Can a mortal man be more righteous than God, or can a man be holier than his Maker?' The voice explained that God does not trust His own servants, and He thinks His angels are foolish. How much less does He regard men who live in a body of clay so fragile that it could be crushed by a tiny moth? God destroys the wicked. They are brought down and die without discovering the meaning of life.

"Job, that is the vision I saw, and here is the interpretation. You have foolishly tried to be more righteous than God. You are beyond help. Not even a saint could help you. Anger and envy kill. God saw you, a foolish man, begin to prosper; so He cursed your family. Because of this curse, your harvest has been eaten by the hungry, choked by thorns, and stolen by robbers. Affliction and trouble happen because wicked men are born to have trouble.

"Job, your problems are proof that you have not been seeking God. God exalts the lowly, saves the poor from the sword, gives hope to the hopeless, and puts an end to iniquity. That is what God is doing to you, putting an end to your sins. Job, you should be singing praise to God because He loves you enough to send all this trouble to chastise you!

"God will deliver you if you will turn to Him. He will bind up your wounds and make you whole. He will protect you from evil, famine, war, gossip, and destruction. You will experience peace. Your children will become great, and you will die an old man, content and at peace.

"Job, this is what I have searched out and found to be true. Listen to me and know these things are for your own good."

Commentary

That was harsh! Job was not a hypocrite or a sinner. Remember, we have the privilege of hearing what was said between God and Satan. But Eliphaz was not allowed to hear God's introduction of Job: "There is none like him in the earth, a perfect and an upright man, one that feareth God, and escheweth evil" (Job 1:8). God knew more about Job than Eliphaz did!

Job's faith had not failed. In fact, faith was all he had left at that point, and his faith prevailed. Job had not compromised his integrity. Innocent people do die, and righteous people do suffer. Trouble does not mean that you have sinned. God is not a cruel God Who destroys men for pleasure. He is very loving and caring.

Dreams and visions do not necessarily mean that God has spoken. There are many instances in the Bible of men having dreams and visions that were either Satanic in origin or a product of their own idealism or ambition. Deuteronomy 13:1-5 warns:

> If there arise among you a prophet, or a dreamer of dreams, and giveth thee a sign or a wonder, And the sign or the wonder come to pass, whereof he spake unto thee, saying, Let us go after other gods, which thou hast not known, and let us serve them; Thou shalt not hearken unto the words of that prophet, or that dreamer of dreams: for the LORD your God proveth you, to know whether ye love the LORD your God with all your heart and with all your soul. Ye shall walk after the LORD your God, and fear him, and keep his commandments, and obey his voice, and ye shall serve him, and cleave unto him. And that prophet, or that dreamer of dreams, shall be put to death; because he hath spoken to turn you away from the LORD your God . . . to thrust thee out of the way which the LORD thy God commanded thee to walk in. So shalt thou put the evil away from the midst of thee."

For dreams and visions to be considered of God, they must be anointed by the Holy Spirit. The disciple Peter told the people of Judea, "In the last days, saith God, I will pour out of my Spirit upon all flesh" (Acts 2:17). The vision of Eliphaz does not sound like that kind of vision but a figment of his own imagination used to scare Job into believing a false doctrine. Never accept a dream or a vision without first checking to see if it lines up with the Bible!

The destiny of man is not gloomy if he knows the Lord. The trouble in this life will be replaced with total peace and joy when we get home. No one is beyond help. Sometimes, believers are not much help, but we have a Father Who cares very much and has promised to be with us in times of trouble. Even the vilest sinner can be washed pure by the blood of Jesus.

Men will have trouble in this life. Job's problems were not the chastening of the Almighty; they were the result of being born into a sinful world. Being a Christian is no guarantee of a life free from trouble. We need to hear the Word of God more than the speeches of man.

CHAPTER FIVE
I Am Not a Hypocrite

JOB'S ACCOUNT
JOB 6:1–7:21

I wish I could make my friends understand that my problem is not sin. I am grieving! Why can't they offer comfort instead of a lecture?

"Oh, Eliphaz, I wish you could understand my grief and feel the depth of my pain! The weight I feel is heavier than wet sand on my chest, choking my ability to form a coherent sentence. God has taken away everything that was special to me, shooting at me with poison darts. The terrors of God are lined up against me.

"Life is flavorless, like eating unsalted food or egg whites. I wish God would just kill me! I have no strength, no hope, no help. I would need strength greater than stones and flesh tougher than brass to survive. I think I am going insane!

"You, my friend, should be ashamed for not showing pity to a friend. Your first words of comfort were refreshing but quickly gave way to insults. I was a weary traveler hoping to find cool, refreshing water only to find an empty, dry gulch. You speak pretty words; but in the face of trouble, you need more than fancy talking points. I never asked for your help, but I would gladly listen if you would speak the truth. Right words are powerful, but arguing is worthless.

"Eliphaz, look at me. You have been my friend a long time, and you would know if I were lying. Please reconsider your arguments. I am righteous, and you cannot prove otherwise.

"Death sounds like the sweetest solution to my problems. I cannot sleep, lying awake all night tossing and turning, waiting for the dawn. My body is crawling with worms, covered with dirt, and running with sore boils. There is no hope for me. The days go by in a blur, faster than the click of knitting needles. Life is as unstable and unpredictable as the wind. I will never see good again.

"Eliphaz, you are beginning to irritate me. I refuse to shut up about my anguish. You are staring at me as if I were a freak. You scare me with dreams and visions. Please, leave me alone to live out the rest of my worthless days in peace and quiet!

"Eliphaz, you are trying to play God. Why have you taken an interest in my situation? Why do you visit me every morning only to judge me? Okay, I will confess: I have sinned. What should I do? If you are so holy and righteous, pardon my sin and take it away!"

Commentary

Job's problem was not sin but grief, and the burden of justifying himself to his friend was just an additional layer of pain. Job strained his imagination to come up with images to describe the hurt Eliphaz's accusations of hypocrisy had caused: wet sand, poison darts, unsalted egg whites.

Job was willing to listen to right words but would never admit that his pain and suffering was caused by sin. Eliphaz knew Job's lifestyle and had no right to accuse him. Since Eliphaz was trying to play God, Job confessed, sarcastically begging him for forgiveness only God can give.

CHAPTER SIX
You Deserve Punishment

BILDAD'S ACCOUNT
JOB 8:1-22

It's time that I step in. Eliphaz is not getting the point across, and I love a good argument!

"Job, you are not making any sense! God makes no mistakes. He is a God of justice; and you deserve everything that has happened to you, including the death of your children. Your sin brought about your destruction.

"You have forgotten the traditions handed down by your fathers, and you have forgotten God. Because of your hypocrisy, you will wither and die. You appear holy, but you have lost contact with God. Your hope will collapse under the slightest pressure.

"Job, God is going to destroy you, then deny that you ever existed. He will get so much enjoyment plucking you up so that others can grow in your place. He does not cast away perfect men, and He will not help sinners. Repent so that God can restore your joy and discredit your enemies."

Commentary

What cruel remarks Bildad makes to one who is suffering! It is true that men do not deserve the blessings of God, but Bildad is saying that Job does not deserve God's blessings because he is a sinner. As we have already seen, that is not the case. To use the tragic death of Job's children to gain debate points is doubly cruel. What a horrible perspective Bildad has about God!

Bildad urges him to return to the tradition of the fathers in order to be blessed. How much better it is to seek God than the traditions of men. Much of the tradition is petty and frivolous, if not actually harmful, in our search for God. Many have been so blinded by erroneous teachings that they cannot see the truth. We should examine our traditions and honor only those which are true to God's Word and which bring honor to the Father.

Jesus admonished against this in Matthew 15:1-9 when speaking to the scribes and Pharisees:

> Then came to Jesus scribes and Pharisees, which were of Jerusalem, saying, Why do thy disciples transgress the tradition of the elders? for they wash not their hands when they eat bread. But he answered and said unto them, Why do ye also transgress the commandment of God *by your tradition?* For God commanded, saying, Honour thy father and mother: and, He that curseth father or mother, let him die the death. But ye say, Whosoever shall say to his father or his mother, It is a gift, by whatsoever thou mightest be profited by me; And honour not his father or his mother, he shall be free. Thus have ye made the commandment of God of none effect *by your tradition.* Ye hypocrites, well did Esaias prophesy of you, saying, This people draweth nigh unto me with their mouth, and honoureth me with their lips; but their heart is far from me. But in vain they do worship me, teaching for doctrines the commandments of men" (emphasis mine).

Bildad claimed that God was asleep and must be awakened, but he must not know the God I know. Psalm 121:3-4 says, "He that keepeth thee will not slumber. Behold, he that keepeth Israel shall neither slumber nor sleep." In fact, there have been many times I paced the floors worrying when God said, "You go on to bed. I'll stay up," or, "You get some rest. No need for both of us to be awake."

Bildad also said that God prospers the righteous; but if that is true, drug lords must be holy men of God. Hitler must have been a saint. People who embezzle millions of dollars must be doing the work of the Kingdom.

The fact is that good people get sick. Righteous men have problems. "Many are the afflictions of the righteous: but the LORD delivereth him out of them all" (Psalm 34:19). The difference is that godly people have the presence of God and the leading of the Holy Spirit to direct them and comfort them during those hard times.

Perhaps you are going through a period of testing and trial right now. Do not allow Satan or your friends to put you down or convince you that you are a sinner just because everything is off-kilter. Put your trust in the God Who promises to walk with you even through "the valley of the shadow of death" (Psalm 23:4) and to "never leave thee, nor forsake thee" (Heb. 13:5).

CHAPTER SEVEN
God Is My Judge

JOB'S ACCOUNT
JOB 9:1-10:22

I am bewildered. Why am I being attacked by my friends when I am already suffering? What is going on here? Bildad is waiting for a response, so I guess I had better say something.

"Bildad, you are right. God does not make mistakes, and hypocrites will be destroyed. But that truth does not apply to me because I have not sinned; I understand God better than you do.

"I have longed for God to speak to me with an audible voice, to send a lightning bolt or some other display of His power to strengthen my faith. In the blackness of night, I have wanted to see God and hear His voice; but I have learned just to trust Him in the silence.

"God is wise and mighty. He is so powerful, He can remove mountains! He could shake the Earth out of its orbit or prevent the sun from rising. He spreads out the heavens and walks on waves. Mere mortals can never comprehend His power.

"Bildad, I recognize my helplessness before God. I know that He is near me. But if I cannot perceive Him, how can I answer Him? The only thing I could do is ask mercy of the great Judge. Even if God spoke, I would not believe that He had heard *my* voice.

"God has broken me for no apparent reason. He will not allow me to catch my breath. He has filled me with bitterness. I cannot justify myself to Him. All my actions prove my sin. Even if I were perfect, I would not understand my soul.

"So, I will admit my lack of understanding. Yes, there are times when it seems that God is not fair in His dealings. And I will admit my cowardice. My days pass in a blur, and I see no good times ahead.

"Time races by so quickly. When I try to find some comfort, I get scared. God is condemning me. My labor is in vain, and I cannot stay clean because God keeps throwing me back into the ditch.

"It is impossible for God and man to come together. There is no one who can can lay his hands on both of us to bridge the gap separating us. Only then could I talk to God without fear!

"I am weary of life. Since there is no mediator, I must speak to God out of the bitterness of my heart. Does He despise me? Why is He fighting with me? What sin have I committed? Who can deliver me from my anguish?

Turning from Bildad, I begin to pray out loud, "Lord, You know me. The hands that created me are turning me back to dust. Lord, You will not let sin go unpunished, but righteousness does not seem to be much better. I cannot lift up my head. I am confused. My affliction is getting worse. You get angrier and angrier with me. Why did You even let me be born? I would not have to deal with this thing called life.

"Lord, I do not have many days left. Please cease the struggling and leave me alone so that I may find a little comfort before I die."

Commentary

How I would like to put my arms around Job and comfort him for a little while. He seems so pitiful in his loneliness and sorrow. But God is not finished yet, and God knows best. There are so many things I wish Job could know at this point. Job will find out later, but we will go over some of them now.

There *is* a Mediator! "For there is one God, and one mediator between God and men, the man Christ Jesus" (I Tim. 2:5). God knew that the sin of Adam had created a permanent division between Himself and His creation. It would never be possible for a sinful man to come into the presence of a holy God without being destroyed by the brilliance of His glory and the awesomeness of His power.

For a time, God recognized the blood of animals as a covering for sin. Indeed, in the Garden of Eden, God instituted animal sacrifices to cover the sins of Adam and Eve. Under this sacrificial system, a sinner could bring a lamb or other offering to the priest, who would slaughter the animal, sprinkle its blood on the sinner, and burn its carcass on the brazen altar. God would recognize the blood of that animal as a covering for the sins that person had committed.

"For it is not possible that the blood of bulls and of goats should *take away* sins" (Heb. 10:4, emphasis mine). The blood of animals was recognized as a *covering* for sin, but only the blood of Jesus can take away sin. First Peter 1:18-19 says, "Forasmuch as ye know that ye were not redeemed with corruptible things . . . But with the precious blood of Christ, as of a lamb without blemish and without spot." God sent His only Son to die on the cross of Calvary for the remission of our sins.

There on the cross, Jesus reached up one hand to God and the other hand down to man and brought us together through His blood. He became the Go-between, the Mediator for which Job longed. How blessed we are on this side of the cross to have our sins forgiven through the blood of Jesus! How wonderful to know that there was One Who took our place in death so that we can live forever in the presence of God!

God was not angry with Job. Job could not know about the contest going on in Heaven. He could not know how God really felt about him. He recognized the power and majesty of God. He believed that God had created him, but he could not know that the Almighty, omnipotent God of the universe loved him as a father loves his son. But you and I can know. As John

3:16-17 says, "For God so loved the world, that he gave his only begotten Son, that whosoever believeth in him should not perish, but have everlasting life. For God sent not his Son into the world to condemn the world; but that the world through him might be saved." God loves you enough to die for you!

God is not the Author of pain and sorrow, of suffering and heartache. We can see from chapter one that Satan is the main source of evil. "The thief cometh not, but for to steal, and to kill, and to destroy: I am come that they might have life, and that they might have it more abundantly" (John 10:10). "Be sober, be vigilant; because your adversary the devil, as a roaring lion, walketh about, seeking whom he may devour" (I Peter 5:8). Satan is the enemy, not God.

We must remember that Satan cannot afflict us without God's permission. I do not pretend to understand why God allows some of the things He does, but I believe God has a plan and a purpose for each of our lives; and when we walk in faith and obedience to Him, He will bring us forth victorious in the end. "And we know that all things work together for good to them that love God, to them who are the called according to his purpose" (Rom. 8:28).

In the last verse of chapter ten, Job bemoans the fact that he is going to a place of darkness. If he could only know what you and I know—that "to be absent from the body [is] to be present with the Lord" (II Cor. 5:8). Where the Lord is, there is no darkness. "And there shall be no night there; and they need no candle, neither light of the sun; for the LORD God giveth them light: and they shall reign for ever and ever" (Rev. 22:5). "And the city had no need of the sun, neither of the moon, to shine in it: for the glory of God did lighten it, and the Lamb is the light thereof" (Rev. 21:23). We are not going to a place of darkness but to a place of radiant light from the One Who is the Light!

CHAPTER EIGHT
You Are Lying

ZOPHAR'S ACCOUNT
JOB 11:1-20

I cannot sit idle any longer and allow these other two to continue speaking to Job. I must interject!

"Should I let your flood of lies continue as you mock God? No, I am going to set the record straight! Job, you will never be able to cover your sins by an avalanche of words. You are a liar, and I will not hold my peace! You are a mocker, and I will shame you into repentance!

"There are three opinions here, Job. There is your opinion. You think that your doctrine is pure; you think you are holy, but you are a sinner. Your opinion is all wrong! Your philosophy stinks! Then, there is God's opinion. Oh, how I wish God would speak and show you how wrong you are. He is not punishing you half enough for your sins. You deserve so much more than you are getting.

"But since God is not speaking, allow me to tell you what He thinks. Your opinion is wrong. So now, listen to me! You cannot find God by searching for Him. You will never understand the Almighty. You talk about being perfect, but the perfection of God is out of your reach.

"God works, and no one can stop Him. If you are arrested, put in prison, or sentenced to death, God did that; and you must not presume to fight against God. God knows vain men like you, and He sees all your wickedness.

"Let me outline for you four steps to restoration: First, you must prepare your heart toward God. Your heart is cold, and you are far away from God. You must come back to God. Then, reach out to God. You made a fine speech about longing for God, but you have not reached out to Him. Open your arms wide, and God will come to you. The third step is to put away your sin. Your protestations of innocence are lies. God only punishes sinners. He does not allow the righteous to suffer this way. And finally, keep sin out of your house. Do not live with wickedness. Righteousness is the only guarantee of blessing.

"My dear Job, if you will follow these four steps to restoration, I promise you will get good results. Your skin will clear. The boils on your body will be healed, and there will not be so much as a spot left on you. You will be steady and unafraid. You confessed that you are afraid and insecure. That bad confession is your problem. You should never confess fear or sickness or doubt. However, by following my four steps, you will find a steadiness to your life. You will become fearless, unafraid to face anything that comes your way.

"You will also forget your misery. When you return to God, He will lift His curse from you and bring you prosperity. You will feel young again. You will have the strength and stamina of a middle-aged man. You will be in the prime of your life—no longer an old, decrepit shell of a man. You will be secure in hope. You will not need to fear anything, and you will be able to sleep at night. People will again seek your advice and wisdom. Your name will be in the community and perhaps in the world!

"But let me give you a final warning. The wicked will be punished and will die without hope. You are going to face the judgment of God!"

Commentary

What a pompous know-it-all! This guy certainly has no problem with self-esteem! Many of the things Zophar said are true—and I would never belittle the truth—but most of them are out of context where Job is concerned.

Zophar exalts God and says that they did not even know half of God's glory and majesty. "Eye hath not seen, nor ear heard, neither have entered into the heart of man, the things which God hath prepared for them that love him" (I Cor. 2:9). He reminds us that God's perfection is so much higher than man. "For my thoughts are not your thoughts, neither are your ways my ways, saith the LORD. For as the heavens are higher than the earth, so are my ways higher than your ways, and my thoughts than your thoughts" (Isa. 55:8-9). He admits that the work of God cannot be hindered. "These things saith he that is holy, he that is true, he that hath the key of David, he that openeth, and no man shutteth; and shutteth, and no man openeth" (Rev. 3:7). Let us never forget that God is Sovereign and can do whatever He pleases.

But there are a couple of things about which Zophar is dead wrong. He says that man cannot know God—that God is not speaking to His people. King Zedekiah asked the prophet Jeremiah, "Is there any word from the LORD? And Jeremiah said, There is" (Jer. 37:17). God began to reveal Himself in Genesis 1:1 and has given man a progressive revelation of Himself ever since. Every time we read the Bible, we receive more knowledge and revelation of God.

But even more than that, Jesus came in the flesh to reveal God to this world. "Who is the image of the invisible God, the firstborn of every creature" (Col. 1:15). Jesus said to Philip, "He that hath seen me hath seen the Father" (John 14:9). We can know God the Father through His Son, Jesus Christ.

Zophar gives some good advice in his four steps to restoration, but we need to beware lest coming to God be reduced to a ritual. Salvation is not a ritual; it is a relationship. Legalistic people think that by keeping a set of rules, they will be righteous. Some believe that to be saved, a person has to wear their hair a certain way or dress a certain way. I fully believe that when a person is saved, he will look, act, talk, and dress like a Christian. But I also know that a person is saved by grace through faith in the finished work of Jesus Christ on the cross (Eph. 2:8-10). Salvation plus anything else becomes a salvation of works instead of grace.

Finally, Zophar says that the righteous always prosper. We have already discussed the error in this thinking, so let us continue with Job's response.

CHAPTER NINE
I Am Speaking Truth

JOB'S ACCOUNT
JOB 12:1-14:22

I have had it with these guys! They are not here to comfort me but to condemn me!

"You gave your three opinions. I will give my three opinions. You and your companions are, without a doubt, the greatest men on earth," I say sarcastically. "I am not even worthy to kiss your hands. You must be the sum of all the wisdom in the world. I suppose that when you die, all the wisdom in the world will die with you.

My three friends are looking at me now with mouths agape. But I continue.

"Next, let me share my opinion of myself. I understand as much as you do. Everyone knows that I am not inferior to you. I am just a man who has been mocked by his neighbors because I called upon God and He answered me. You laugh me to scorn because I am just and upright. My whole situation disturbs you because it does not fit your theology.

"Finally, let me tell you about my opinion of God. He is constantly revealing Himself to men through creation. His hands have made everything. God gave us ability and perception. He gives wisdom because He is Wisdom, Strength, Counsel, and Understanding. When God breaks something in pieces, no man has the power to re-build it. When He shuts something, no man has the strength to open it. He spoils the wisdom of counselors and turns judges into fools. He deposes kings, destroys mighty men, and silences the wise. He removes understanding from the ancients, pours contempt upon rulers, and weakens the mighty. He causes great leaders to stagger like drunkards. He builds up nations only to tear them down. All men belong to God, and He does with them as He pleases.

"I protest your arrogance. I see, hear, and understand as well as you do. I am not inferior to you! I wish I could talk to God and reason with Him because you are all liars and worthless physicians. If you really want to display your wisdom, then be quiet. To stop this flow of foolish talking would be the wisest thing you could do.

"Please listen to me. When you presume to talk for God, your speech is wicked and deceitful. When you argue on His behalf, you end up mocking Him. You showed compassion when I was well and wealthy; but now, you despise me. God will judge you for your respect of persons. Do you not tremble in His presence when you remember that you are just ashes and clay?

"Please allow me to speak, regardless of the consequences. Trusting in you is like eating my own flesh. I trusted you with my life, and you betrayed me; but there is still One I can depend on. I will trust God even if He kills me! I will continue to walk before Him in righteousness because He is my Salvation.

"My friends, listen to me! I have presented my case before God, and He *will* justify me. I will continue to pray to Him, for it is certain that you cannot plead my cause before God. If I keep silent, I will die! Now, bow with me in prayer.

"Oh, Lord, grant me two requests. First of all, please allay my fear by reducing my afflictions. They are more than I can bear. Second, speak to me and let me answer You; or either let me speak, and You answer. Please, God, speak to me! I have so many questions for You. What sins have I committed? Why do You hide from me and treat me like an enemy? How much more torment must I endure?

"I understand that all men are born into trouble only to be cut down like grass. But why do You judge my insignificant life? Since no one can be clean in Your eyes, why do You hold men responsible for what they have no control over? You have appointed man only a certain number of days and set up restrictions for his life. Please, Lord, let me just live out my few days in rest. Let me finish my day's work and go on to my reward.

"Lord, hide me in the grave until Your anger is past, and then bring me forth again. Oh, God, please remember me!

"Lord, is life really hopeless? Is death as final as it seems? Is there life after death? I am believing for something better than the finality of death. After our appointed days, there will be a resurrection; and You will commune with the people You have created. In the meantime, Lord, please talk to me.

"I suppose my hope of resurrection is foolish. You record every sin, sewing them in a bag I carry on my back. Like the majestic mountains crumble, the hopes of man are relentlessly eroded. You change man's appearance—his skin wrinkles; his hair turns gray; his teeth fall out—and then You toss him aside like a useless piece of junk. He is not allowed to enjoy the success of his children or comfort them when they fail. He is too wrapped up in his own pain. His own misery blots out everything else, and he goes through life absorbed in his own problems."

Commentary

Job has hit rock bottom in his pain and suffering; but before we judge too harshly, we need to remember his situation. He is sitting on the ash heap covered with running sores. He has lost everything he owns, as well as his precious children. His wife has turned against him, wanting him to die and get out of her sight. His three friends have accused him of sinning against God. His situation is proof to them that God has turned His back and no longer cares about him. When all the odds are against you, it is very difficult to remain optimistic.

Job's response to Zophar's speech begins with a delightful display of sarcasm: "No doubt but ye are the people" (Job 12:2). In a mocking tone, he points out their arrogance and self-righteousness.

Job's opinion of God is magnificent! He portrays God as the Creator of all the animals, the One Who holds all of creation in the palm of His hand. God gave man ability, perception, wisdom, and understanding. No power in Heaven or on earth can hinder the work of the Almighty God. He controls the waters—to dry them up or release them. God controls the destiny of men, exalting some and casting down others. God understands all the deep mysteries. In short, He is an awesome God worthy of our respect, adoration, and trust. In a momentous declaration of faith, Job speaks those often-quoted words, "Though he slay me, yet will I trust in him" (Job 13:15). What a marvelous faith Job displays, even in this time of severe testing!

In Job 13:21, Job asks God to withdraw His hand a little and give him some rest. He still believes that God is responsible for all that is happening to him. He did not hear the conversation between God and Satan and is unaware of the source of his problems, yet he maintains his faith in God.

I have often heard that a Christian is not supposed to question God. "Never ask why; just believe." Well, somebody forgot to tell Job the rules. He comes to God with all kinds of questions. Indeed, he sounds like a five-year-old when he starts with the "whys."

Have you ever been tempted to question God? Did you ever just want to look up to the heavens and say, "God, why is this happening? Why did You let this take place?" Or perhaps you have been questioning God, and now you feel guilty. Well, let me tell you what I think. (I sound like one of Job's friends now!) I believe that God allows and even encourages honest questions.

How many parents get angry when their children come with questions? I know you get exasperated with the repetition, but you realize that a child learns by asking questions. It is okay, even when they ask you why you did a certain thing. "Daddy, why did you pour that can of oil in your car? Mommy, why did you put eggs in that cake recipe?" Those questions give us opportunity to teach and explain. I wonder sometimes if God is not waiting for His children to come to Him, tug on His sleeve, and say, "Father, explain why this is happening. Why did You do this?" I am convinced that God not only allows those questions but also uses them to teach His children about His workings and plan for our lives. So, go ahead. Ask! You may never learn until you do.

Job makes a couple of statements with which I disagree, looking from this side of the cross. He said that no one could change from unclean to clean; and while that is true from a human perspective, it is completely false from God's perspective. "Come now, and let us reason together, saith the LORD: though your sins be as scarlet, they shall be as white as snow; though they be red like crimson, they shall be as wool" (Isa. 1:18). Second Corinthians 5:17 says, "Therefore if any man be in Christ, he is a new creature: old things are passed away; behold, all things are become new." And we read in 1 John 1:7, "The blood of Jesus Christ his Son cleanseth us from all sin." Man can turn over a new leaf and make lots of resolutions, but only God can change the heart! God *can* change men from unclean to clean!

Job also said that there is no hope in death; but he is not quite sure, so he asks the question, "If a man die, shall he live again?" From this side of the cross, we have the answer in the resurrection of Jesus Christ from the grave. Jesus said to Mary and Martha standing outside the tomb of their brother Lazarus, "I am the resurrection, and the life: he that believeth in me, though he were dead, yet shall he live: And whosoever liveth and believeth in me shall never die. Believeth thou this?" (John 11:25-26). Then the Resurrection and the Life called for Lazarus to come out of the tomb and presented him back to his sisters.

Paul explains in his writing to the Thessalonians:

> But I would not have you to be ignorant, brethren, concerning them which are asleep, that ye sorrow not, even as others which have no hope. For if we believe that Jesus died and rose again,

even so them also which sleep in Jesus will God bring with him. For this we say unto you by the word of the Lord, that we which are alive and remain unto the coming of the Lord shall not prevent them which are asleep. For the Lord himself shall descend from heaven with a shout, with the voice of the archangel, and with the trump of God: and the dead in Christ shall rise first: Then we which are alive and remain shall be caught up together with them in the clouds, to meet the Lord in the air: and so shall we ever be with the Lord. Wherefore comfort one another with these words" (I Thess. 4:13-18).

Because of the resurrection of Jesus, we have hope that we, too, will be resurrected. But even more exciting is the teaching from Scripture that although the body goes back to the ground after death, the spirit goes into the presence of God. "We are confident, I say, and willing rather to be absent from the body, and to be present with the Lord" (II Cor. 5:8). Job, there is hope—even after death!

This is the end of the first debate with all three friends having a turn to speak and Job offering a rebuttal to each. Job concludes his reply to Zophar with a rather lengthy prayer to God. How wonderful it would have been if these three could have fallen on their knees to join Job in his communion with God! There, in the presence of God on that old ash heap, they could have found reconciliation and forgiveness. When God is present in the midst, controversy ceases; differences are resolved; enemies are reconciled; and peace reigns. What a beautiful ending it would make to this first debate to see those four men with their heads bowed in prayer to the God of Heaven.

Unfortunately, it is not to be. Eliphaz is straining at the bits for Job to say amen so that he can take his next turn. He is not interested in listening to Job or to God—only in his next argument.

CHAPTER TEN
You Are Evil

ELIPHAZ'S ACCOUNT
JOB 15:1-35

"Wrong! Wrong! Wrong! Job, you are wrong!" I say, exasperated. "Your knowledge is useless. Your speeches are worthless. You presume to pray to the very God Who is punishing you. You pray a pretty prayer, but out of your mouth comes wickedness. Your own lies testify against you.

"Job, what gives you the right to approach God? Are you the oldest man alive? Are you the first man to be born? Perhaps you are older than the hills. Perhaps you have heard all of God's secrets and are keeping them to yourself. What do you know that we do not? What do you understand that we seem to be missing? For we are all old enough to be your father. We three are the experienced ones.

"Do you think the consolation of God is a small thing? You are so carried away with pride that you wink and turn away from God. How can you allow yourself to speak such blasphemy? It is impossible for men to be righteous. Job, you make God sick!

"Let me tell you how it is. I will show you what I have seen. Wise men have passed these truths down through the generations, and I will teach them to you.

"Wickedness brings suffering. The prosperity of the sinner will be destroyed. The sinner tries to hide behind his riches only to wax fat and lazy.

He does not trust other people, so he lives alone. But the riches he trusted in will be destroyed. The darkness he loved will consume him.

"Job, you claim to be holy, but it is impossible for a man to be clean in the sight of God. God does not even trust the angels He created and considers the heavens an unclean thing. How much more despicable is a man who consumes iniquity like drinking water. Wicked men suffer in pain all their lives, surrounded by the noise of destruction. They will be consumed by their hypocrisy and bribery will be consumed."

Commentary

Can you imagine mocking someone for praying? Eliphaz is so intent on winning this debate that he will stoop to any level for a slight edge. He says that Job should not pray because he is a sinner. He thinks only righteous people are allowed to call on God! But how blessed we are to be able to call on God, even in our sins.

Jesus told about the proud Pharisee, whose prayer consisted of nothing more than his telling God all about his good deeds. But there was a publican (synonym for "sinner"), who would not lift up so much as his eyes to Heaven, asking, "God be merciful to me a sinner" (Luke 18:13). Jesus said, "I tell you, this man went down to his house justified rather than the other: for every one that exalteth himself shall be abased; and he that humbleth himself shall be exalted" (Luke 18:14). God heard the prayer of a sinner! Thanks be to God that He still hears the humble prayer of repentance.

In fact, Jesus came to this earth for the express purpose of saving sinners. When the Pharisees rebuked Jesus for eating with Matthew, the tax collector (another synonym for "sinner"), Jesus replied, "They that be whole need not a physician, but they that are sick . . . I am not come to call the righteous, but sinners to repentance" (Matt. 9:12-13).

Thanks be to God that He called me one day! I was an old sinner on my way to Hell, lost without a hope in the world; but Jesus called my name. He heard my prayer for forgiveness, washed away my sins, wrote my name in the Book of Life, and put the joy of salvation in my heart! Bless the name of the Lord our God!

Eliphaz implies that since he is old enough to be Job's father, he has more wisdom and experience than Job. But that kind of wisdom comes not from length of days but from knowing God. "The fear of the LORD is the beginning of wisdom: and the knowledge of the holy is understanding" (Prov. 9:10).

The God that Eliphaz teaches about has little regard for man. He does not trust His saints; He thinks the heavens are dirty and that men are abominable and filthy. Now, I realize that men have nothing to offer God. "But we are all as an unclean thing, and all our righteousnesses are as filthy rags" (Isa. 64:6). Man is a depraved creature capable of all kinds of sin and debauchery. The fallen nature of an unregenerate person is filthy.

But the Gospel message says that God loves sinners! "For God so loved the world, that he gave his only begotten Son, that whosoever believeth in him should not perish, but have everlasting life" (John 3:16). "For when we were yet without strength, in due time Christ died for the ungodly . . . But God commendeth his love toward us, in that, while we were yet sinners, Christ died for us" (Rom. 5:6, 8).

Eliphaz has an "I" problem. "*I* will show thee . . . Hear *me* . . . That which *I* have seen . . . *I* will declare . . ." That seems to be the problem. It is not God speaking, but rather Eliphaz who presumes to speak for God.

The prophets of old came thundering, "Thus saith the Lord God." John the Baptist said in true humility, "Behold the Lamb of God, which taketh away the sin of the world . . . He must increase, but I must decrease" (John 1:29, 3:30). It is not our job to lift up ourselves but to point men to Jesus Christ. Much of the problem with denominations, charismatic pastors, and television or radio evangelists is that they tend to draw men to themselves. May we return to such a concern for lost souls that our one desire is to point men to the One Who has power to change their lives. Nobody will be affected by patterning their life after men, but what a difference it makes when they can look to "Jesus, the author and finisher of our faith" (Heb. 12:2).

Once again, Eliphaz states that only the wicked suffer, implying that the suffering of Job was the result of sin. Once again, we must return to chapter one to look at God's opinion of Job—he is a righteous man! Wickedness does not prove sin any more than prosperity proves righteousness.

CHAPTER ELEVEN
You Are Miserable Comforters

JOB'S ACCOUNT
JOB 16:1-14

"Eliphaz, you are all miserable comforters! You talk a good talk; but if our positions were reversed, I could speak the same way to you. But I would rather try to comfort you and understand your pain.

"My pain has made me weary, and you are only making things worse! You miserable comforters have gaped at me as if I were some kind of freak. Your words have punched me in the face like a fist. You have ganged up on me until I am afraid and alone.

"God has delivered me to an ungodly trio of friends. I am shattered, yet He continues to beat me down, shaking me to pieces and using me for target practice. I am in perpetual mourning. My strength is gone, and I sit in the dust like a beggar. I have wept until my face is unrecognizable.

"But I am still innocent! My hands are clean, and my prayer is pure. God is my Witness that my record in Heaven is without offense. While you mock me, I am begging God for relief. I wish there was someone to plead my case before God as my lawyer would plead my case on earth.

"I am dying! My breath smells like death; my days are coming to an end. I am surrounded by mockers who continually provoke me. I have no one who can guarantee my life. I have become a laughingstock, a punching bag for the ungodly. My eyes are filled with tears, and I am just waiting to die. Righteous people should be astonished and angered by my situation. The innocent should fight against the hypocrite. Clean hands should prevail, but it is not so. You foolish accusers are back again to torment me. My life is over; my plans are shattered; and my dreams are crushed. Time is passing so swiftly that night blends into day. All hope is gone."

Commentary

It is so easy to criticize and so hard to empathize. In dealing with suffering people, we need to try to get inside their skin—to really understand from where they are coming. There is an old saying that admonishes, "Don't judge a man until you have walked a mile in his shoes." Job's friends think they are helping, but they are causing untold misery and anguish of spirit to Job. He is already in a desperate struggle with depression and doubt without the added weight of criticism and the false doctrines of his friends.

Job reminds us that it is easy to give advice when we are not the one in trouble. We can look down our self-righteous noses at those who are less fortunate and judge them for their sins or failures. *All those homeless people should get jobs and buy a home. Everyone infected with AIDS deserves to die and go to Hell. Do not get too close to the alcoholic and the prostitute, lest they contaminate you.* People by the thousands all around us are going to Hell, while we sit in our fancy churches with carpeted floors and padded seats. We serve God by keeping our hands uncontaminated by the scum of the earth. But I wonder what our Father will say when we stand before Him on the Day of Judgment.

It seems to me that the words of Jesus are very appropriate:

> Then shall he say also unto them on the left hand, Depart from me, ye cursed, into everlasting fire, prepared for the devil and his angels: For I was an hungered, and ye gave me no meat: I was thirsty, and ye gave me no drink: I was a stranger, and

ye took me not in: naked, and ye clothed me not: sick, and in prison, and ye visited me not. Then shall they also answer him, saying, Lord, when saw we thee an hungered, or athirst, or a stranger, or naked, or sick, or in prison, and did not minister unto thee? Then shall he answer them, saying, Verily I say unto you, Inasmuch as ye did it not to one of the least of these, ye did it not to me (Matt. 25:41-45).

May the God of mercy give us eyes to see others with the love of God. May He give us the compassion of our Lord Jesus as we encounter the hurting and downtrodden of this life. Those on the ash heap need an expression of love instead of criticism.

Job said that his record was in Heaven. What a beautiful thought during criticism. It is not the record of men that matter but the record of God. When men would condemn us to Hell, God shows us love. When the record of this world would sentence us to death, God, in His undeserved mercy, wipes the slate clean and allows us to start over. "And you, being dead in your sins and the uncircumcision of your flesh, hath he quickened together with him, having forgiven you all trespasses; Blotting out the handwriting of ordinances that was against us, which was contrary to us, and took it out of the way, nailing it to his cross" (Col. 2:13-14).

When Satan comes to accuse you of the sins of your past, send him to the Father. In the record book of Heaven, your list of sins has been purged by the blood of Jesus, and you stand justified in the sight of God without any charges against you. God has taken all of those confessed sins and thrown them away from Him "as far as the east is from the west" (Psalm 103:12), never to be remembered against you anymore! Your record is clean, and do not ever let the devil forget it!

Once again, Job longs for someone to plead his case before God. How thankful we should be for the knowledge of our Divine Lawyer, Who pleads our case before the Father.

Seeing then that we have a great high priest, that is passed into the heavens, Jesus the Son of God, let us hold fast our profession. For we have not an high priest which cannot be touched with the feeling of our infirmities; but was in all points tempted like as we are, yet without sin. Let us therefore come boldly unto the throne of grace, that we may obtain mercy, and find grace to help in time of need . . . Wherefore he is able also to save them to the uttermost that come unto God by him, seeing he ever liveth to make intercession for them (Heb. 4:14-16, 7:25).

Think of Jesus, your High Priest, leaning over to the Father, pleading your case. Luke 22:31-32 tells us, "Satan hath desired to have you, that he may sift you as wheat: But I have prayed for thee, that thy faith fail not."

CHAPTER TWELVE
You Are Going to Hell

BILDAD'S ACCOUNT
JOB 18:1-21

"Job, there are just two things wrong with you—you talk too much, and you are a sinner! Let me know when you stop talking so that I can speak. Why do you call us foolish? You are tearing yourself apart in your anger, but it accomplishes nothing.

"If you were righteous, things would be different. Job, no one believes your 'innocent' testimony anymore. Everyone can see that you are not righteous. You have been given over to darkness, and it will only get worse. You will walk into a trap, be ambushed by thieves, and chased by your enemies.

"You will be terrified because you no longer belong to God or have His protection on your life. Your strength will fail; destruction will consume you. Your confidence will fail, and terror will reign over you as a king. You will be filled with burning brimstone. No one will remember your name. You will leave behind no heirs to carry on your name. Everyone will be astonished at your destruction. Darkness will devour you as you are chased out of this world. Surely, the pit is the fate of all the wicked and the final resting place for those who do not know God. Job, you are on that slippery road to Hell."

Commentary

Bildad would make a good evangelist—he knows how to scare the life out of a person! But as is so often the case, he is preaching to the converted. Job is not guilty. He has not forsaken God, and the things that have come upon him are not the result of sin.

The apostle John talks about a man who had been blind from birth. The disciples of Jesus jumped to the same conclusion as Job's friends. "Master, who did sin, this man, or his parents, that he was born blind?" (John 9:2). Centuries later, they still have not learned that you cannot judge people that way. The old idea is still there: "If you are suffering, you are a sinner. If you are healthy and wealthy, you are righteous." Again, let me remind you that if prosperity equals righteousness, the men who are selling drugs to your children are godly men doing the work of the Father.

We need to hear the reply of our Lord to the question of His disciples (and to Job's friends): "Neither hath this man sinned, nor his parents: but that the works of God should be made manifest in him" (John 9:3). Jesus proceeded to manifest the work of God by healing the man of his blindness, proving that the man's blindness was not caused by sin.

Please, if you learn nothing else from the book of Job, learn not to judge people harshly when they are going through suffering and pain. Rather, show them the love of God and reach out a hand to help, if possible. At any rate, pray for God to minister to their needs and give them grace to make it through their particular valley.

If you cannot help, please refrain from tearing them down. The accusation that no one believed his testimony anymore must have cut Job deeply. A person who truly loves God desires a good testimony before the world. Jesus said, "Let your light so shine before men, that they may see your good works, and glorify your Father which is in heaven" (Matt. 5:16). To have that light smeared and taken lightly wounds the soul.

Let us dwell just a moment on a good point that Bildad makes—anger will tear you apart and accomplish nothing. The worst thing a person can do is internalize anger; for somewhere along the way, it will break out and quite literally tear you apart. Everyone needs to find constructive ways of releasing anger—take a walk, count to ten (or one hundred!), or perform a physical chore to relieve tension. Then when things are calmer, talk it out. Find a good listener and pour it all out. You will see more clearly and perhaps come to some rational solutions.

One of the best things Bildad could have done for Job was to listen to him and let him express his pain, anguish, and confusion. But typically, Bildad was not interested in listening; he was interested in talking.

CHAPTER THIRTEEN
I Have a Redeemer!

JOB'S ACCOUNT
JOB 19:1–29

"Bildad, you are irritating me with your words! These ten times you have criticized me and treated me as an enemy. What if I have sinned? It is absolutely none of your business! It is my problem and not yours! Let me tell you something—God is doing a better job at working against me than you ever could!

"I scream and cry, but He does not hear me. I cannot escape catastrophe. I stumble in the darkness. God has taken away my glory, plucked me up like a tree, and dashed all my hopes. God is angry with me and counts me as an enemy. There is no escape.

"My friends have turned against me, and my own family has turned their back on me. Even those of my own house count me as a stranger—my maid looks at me like I am some kind of alien; my servant refuses to answer me, even when I threaten him; and my wife thinks I am repulsive. I begged her to have other children to carry on my name, but she turned up her nose and would not let me come near her. Everyone has abandoned me. Even my body has failed me. I am nothing but skin and bones.

"Please, someone have pity on me. Please, just be my friend. I need your help and support. Why do you insist on persecuting me? Must you add to my pain and suffering by your criticism? Why do you continue to persecute me and wish me dead?

"Write this down before I die! For suddenly, I know! I have caught a glimpse of life beyond my troubles. With the eyes of faith, I see what is ahead! My Redeemer lives! He is alive and working on my behalf both now and forever. At the end of time, He shall stand on the earth with His saints. Even when my body dies, I will see God in my resurrected body. I will see Him for myself!

"And you, my so-called friends, instead of persecuting me, you should examine yourselves in the fear of God. He is coming with the sword of judgment to punish the wicked."

Commentary

Have you ever felt the glory and the presence of God sweep into a place? You are in an ordinary worship service when suddenly, you sense the Holy Spirit. You are driving down the road meditating on God when His very presence floods the interior of your car. You are walking along the road of sorrow and despair when you hear the soft sound of sandaled feet beside you. In a moment, you go from gloom to glory. The clouds roll back, and sunshine floods your soul. The burdens float away, and your spirit soars. For a moment, you stand on the mountaintop of faith, where nothing is impossible and you catch a brief glimpse of things from God's perspective.

You can discern the moment that same presence of God suddenly comes upon Job. Sitting on the ash heap, covered with boils, bemoaning his loss, surrounded by the criticism of his friends, Job becomes aware of "the fourth man in the fire" (Dan. 3), of the angel in the lion's den (Dan. 6), of the Stranger "who talked with us by the way" (Luke 24:32). Suddenly, Job is not alone with his problems. They have all but disappeared as he catches a revelation from God concerning the future.

Job has been badly stung by the words of his friends. Whoever said "words will never harm me" was lying. Word wounds are the most deadly and poisonous. The criticism of a friend can cut to the bone, deflating the ego of the most self-assured.

Job admitted that the criticism of his friends had broken him into pieces. He says that they have reproached him ten times. Since there have only been five speeches thus far, each speech has been a two-edged sword cutting both ways.

May God teach us to be careful with the words of our mouth. Proverbs 18:21 warns us, "Death and life are in the power of the tongue." And Matthew 12:37 reminds us, "For by thy words thou shalt be justified, and by thy words thou shalt be condemned." "A word fitly spoken is like apples of gold in pictures of silver" (Prov. 25:11).

Job accused his friends of magnifying themselves against him in his hour of need. There are many who need to exalt themselves at the expense of others, to step on the fallen to reach their next rung of the ladder of success. Some would take advantage of the misfortunes of others to better themselves, but that is not the way of those who love God and are seeking to please Him. God teaches us to remember the poor and needy and to minister to them if it is in our power to do so. Proverbs 19:17 says, "He that hath pity upon the poor lendeth unto the LORD; and that which he hath given will he pay him again." God will reward those who minister to others.

Job thought all hope was gone. The destroyer had come and taken away everything, "and I am escaped with the skin of my teeth" (Job 19:20). You thought that phrase was a modern invention, but it is thousands of years old.

But all his complaints are forgotten as the presence of God invades the ash heap. The anointing of the Holy Ghost breathes a spark of holy fire into Job's spirit, and his faith soars to the mountaintop. Thanks be to God that in the moment of trial and testing, there is always knowledge of God's presence. "For he hath said, I will never leave thee, nor forsake thee" (Heb. 13:5). Matthew 28:20 says, "And, lo, I am with you always, even unto the end of the world." Even when we walk in the pain and the darkness, we have the assurance that God our Helper is with us. As it says in Psalm 23:4, "Yea, though I walk through the valley of the shadow of death, I will fear no evil: for thou art with me."

But sometimes, it is more than just assurance. Sometimes, God explodes the darkness with showers of His glory. Every once and a while, He takes us into that secret place where only the saints can go to reveal a portion of Himself that so astounds, electrifies, and uplifts that we forget all else. We gaze on His holy face and bask in His presence, leaving the cares of the world far behind. There in His presence comes the light of revelation. Suddenly, we just know!

Job had asked the question about life after death, but there on the mountaintop of faith, he knew the answer. "*I know* that my redeemer liveth" (Job 19:25). He received revelation about a coming Redeemer. But more than a Redeemer, there would be One Who is near of kin. The Hebrew word is *gaal*, which means "to be the next of kin."

Job, looking across the centuries of time, saw the Son of Man hanging on an old, rugged cross to pay the redemption price for all mankind. Thanks be to God that we have been redeemed. First Peter 1:18-19 tells us, "Forasmuch as ye know that ye were not redeemed with corruptible things, as silver and gold . . . But with the precious blood of Christ, as of a lamb without blemish and without spot." The debt we owed has been paid in full by the blood of the spotless Lamb of God. The penalty of death has been paid for, and we are free. "If the Son therefore shall make you free, ye shall be free indeed" (John 8:36).

Job also had a revelation of a Conqueror Who would stand on the earth in the latter day. Not only is the Redeemer living now, but He will also reign at the end of the age. In Revelation, we see the angels declaring that all the kingdoms of the earth have been given to Christ, Who shall reign for ever and ever. (Rev. 11:15-17) He is called "KING OF KINGS, AND LORD OF LORDS" (Rev. 19:11-16).

In addition to the revelation of a coming Redeemer and a reigning Conqueror, Job saw a revelation of the bodily resurrection of the saints from the dead. "And though after my skin worms destroy this body, yet *in my flesh* shall I see God" (Job 19:26). What a remarkable revelation for a man living probably four thousand years before Christ was born.

Yes, there is life after death! As I Corinthians 15:42-44 says, "So also is the resurrection of the dead. It is sown in corruption; it is raised in incorruption: It is sown in dishonour; it is raised in glory: it is sown in weakness; it is raised in power: It is sown a natural body; it is raised a spiritual body" (I Cor. 15:42-44).

When a person dies, his spirit goes immediately into the presence of God in Heaven, and his body goes back to the ground. At the rapture of the Church, the souls of all those who died in Christ will return with Him to be reunited with their resurrected bodies (I Thess. 4:13-18).

Not only is my Redeemer alive, but I shall also see Him for myself in the resurrection of the dead! Let the worms devour my flesh, and let my strength be consumed—this is not the end!

And finally, Job had a revelation of the coming judgment. Saints will be judged at the Judgment Seat of Christ for the deeds done in their body. Some will be crowned with the crown of faithfulness, the crown of soul-winning, the crown of righteousness, etc.; but all will receive the crown of life. "Be thou faithful unto death, and I will give thee a crown of life" (Rev. 2:10). I am working for a crown—not because I deserve it, but in order to have something to lay at the feet of Jesus (Rev. 4:9-11).

On that day, I want to be able to take what little crown I have received and lay it down at His feet, proclaiming that I am not worthy to wear it. Only my Lord Jesus Christ is worthy! Jesus will be wearing all the crowns of the saints when He comes back to earth to reign.

But there is also coming a judgment for those who reject the blood of Jesus: the Great White Throne Judgment. All sinners will stand before God to be condemned to everlasting torment. If you are not saved, may the Spirit of God draw you now to believe on the name of the Lord Jesus before it is too late.

CHAPTER FOURTEEN
You Have Robbed the Poor

ZOPHAR'S ACCOUNT
JOB 20:1-29

"Job, I could hardly wait to speak when I heard your insults. Since the beginning of time, wicked men have only enjoyed short triumphs. They die and are forgotten, and any fleeting success is lost.

"Job, you are that wicked hypocrite! When our children gave to the poor you took it back. You are a perpetual sinner from childhood until death. God will cause you to vomit up the riches you have accumulated. You will not prosper because only the righteous prosper.

"Job, you have oppressed the poor. Your wealth has been accumulated by fraud, confiscating homes you did not build. You will never be able to enjoy the work of your hands or have peace in your wickedness. Everything you have will be destroyed because this is how God punishes the wicked. This is the heritage which God has appointed to the sinner."

Commentary

Zophar admits that he could hardly wait to burst Job's bubble. How he longed to bring Job down from the mountaintop of revelation back to the ash heap, back to the topic at hand. When you make a move to draw closer to God, there will always be those who will try to pull you back down to earth. "Let's not get too emotional. Don't go off the deep end with this religion bit. Go to church on Sunday, but don't try to bring your religion to work on Monday. The world operates on different rules."

Unfortunately, it is not always those outside the church who try to tear you down. Many so-called saints will get jealous or angry when you begin to show more spiritual maturity than they. "Who does he think he is? I have been saved a lot longer than he has, and I have never experienced God in that way. It must be of the devil."

Moses was handpicked by God to lead the children of Israel out of Egyptian bondage. He had seen the burning bush, stood up to Pharaoh, assumed the heartaches of leading one-and-a-half million people through the wilderness, spent forty days and nights with God on the top of Mount Sinai to receive the law; and yet there were those who wanted His glory without paying His price. They wanted their own face to shine without spending time with God. They were jealous of the authority God had given to Moses. "And they gathered themselves together against Moses and against Aaron, and said unto them, Ye take too much upon you, seeing all the congregation are holy, every one of them, and the LORD is among them: wherefore then lift ye up yourselves above the congregation of the LORD?" (Num. 16:3).

Moses prayed, and God answered in a spectacular fashion. "And the earth opened her mouth, and swallowed them up, and their houses, and all the men that appertained unto Korah, and all their goods. They, and all that appertained to them, went down alive into the pit, and the earth closed upon them: and they perished from among the congregation" (Num. 16:32-33).

Perhaps God will not revenge you as quickly or as spectacularly as he did Moses; but God is on your side, and He will take care of all your enemies in His own time and in His own way. The important thing is to not seek vengeance yourself but to leave it all in the hands of God and continue serving Him with all your heart. Seek to mature in Christ, even if nobody else approves!

Zophar said, "The spirit of *my* understanding causeth me to answer" (Job 20:3). How much better to wait for the understanding of God before he opened his mouth. As Proverbs 3:5-6 says, "Trust in the LORD with all thine heart; and lean not unto thine own understanding. In all thy ways acknowledge him, and he shall direct thy paths" (Prov. 3:5-6).

Despite his impulsiveness, much of what Zophar said is true. Sin will be punished. The wicked will perish, and there is coming a judgment day for all those who reject God. The Bible tells us, "For the wages of sin is death" (Rom. 6:23). "And sin, when it is finished, bringeth forth death" (James 1:15).

The only problem with Zophar's speech is his assumption that Job is wicked because of his pain and suffering. What he said is true, but it just does not apply to Job.

CHAPTER FIFTEEN
The Wicked Are Allowed to Prosper

JOB'S ACCOUNT
JOB 21:1-34

"Zophar, listen. After I am finished talking, you will get another chance to mock me. Please put your hand over your mouth to keep it quiet.

"I am afraid. I sit here trembling at your lie—wicked men *do* prosper. They live to old age and become powerful. They see their children and their grandchildren become successful. They are safe from fear, not feeling the punishment of God. Their herds increase; and their children are happy. Wicked men enjoy their wealth all the way to the grave, saying to God, 'Leave us alone. There is no reason for us to serve the Almighty. There is no profit in prayer.'

"Yes, some wicked men do not prosper. Often, God sends sorrow and destruction their way in this lifetime. Their children suffer for their fathers' sins. What little pleasure they have known is temporary; for their life is cut short, and they go to an early grave. The point is, some wicked prosper; and some do not because God is the Judge.

Some sinners die full of strength, at ease, at peace, and prosperous. Some sinners die bitter and sad, never having known pleasure. But they both die! Ride along the road and look at the houses along the way. You cannot tell which ones belong to the righteous and which ones belong to the wicked. But be assured that the wicked will be judged—whether in his lifetime or in the grave. Everybody before him has died, and everybody after him will die, too. You have tried to comfort me in vain, for your answers are all lies."

Commentary

Zophar was only the first to pervert the doctrine of prayer which Jesus taught: "And in that day ye shall ask me nothing. Verily, verily, I say unto you, Whatsoever ye shall ask the Father in my name, he will give it you" (John 16:23). Those words are God-breathed, Holy Ghost-inspired, and powerful in their context; but some have used them to equate prosperity with the blessings of God and poverty with sin. God does provide for our needs, but He does not give us the authority to pray for frivolous things to satisfy our greed. God gives us what we pray for when we pray in His name and according to His will. We must learn to want the "whatevers" that God wants.

Job pointed out that you cannot tell sinners from saints by their bank accounts, the cars they drive, the houses they live in, on the condition of their health. If that were true, drug lords, corrupt politicians, and trust fund babies would be super saints, while the poor missionary barely scraping by would be a condemned sinner. How absurd!

Judgment does not always come in this life, but all will be judged based solely on their relationship with Jesus Christ. We might give an account for how we used our money but not for being rich or poor.

CHAPTER SIXTEEN
You Mistreat Orphans

ELIPHAZ'S ACCOUNT
JOB 22:1-30

"Job, you think you are God's pet, but you are not half as profitable to God as you think you are. Do you think God is jumping up and down with joy over the fact that you, Mr. High-and-Mighty, claim to be a righteous person? Is your perfection making God rich? Or maybe you think because you are so smart that God is going to let you sit in judgment with Him.

"Let me set the record straight. You are a self-righteous hypocrite whose wickedness and iniquities are without number. You have defrauded your own brother. You have taken away clothes from the naked. You refuse water to the weary and withhold bread from the hungry. You grovel before powerful men, but you send widows away empty and break the arms of orphans.

"But be assured, Job, that God's judgment is upon you. You think God is so high in the Heaven that He cannot see you. You think the clouds will prevent God's judgment from reaching you. You think God is too busy to notice your sins. But you had better think again about the ways of wicked men. God kills them prematurely or washes them away in a flood. God blesses them with good things but takes away their ability to enjoy their blessings.

"You could join an elite group of merrymakers if you would only turn to God. Get acquainted with Him, and He will give you peace and prosperity.

Receive the Word of the Lord, return to the Almighty, put away sin; and the blessings of God will rain upon you abundantly.

"God will defend you from all your enemies and give you an abundance. As you delight in God, He will answer every prayer and pay all your vows. Every word you speak will be established as truth. There will be no more darkness or fear. You will be able to encourage those who are depressed and in despair. You could be a blessing instead of a reproach."

Commentary

No more Mr. Nice Guy for Eliphaz! There is enough venom here to kill a bull elephant! Eliphaz is angry because his theology has been challenged. He thinks God punishes all the wicked and blesses all the righteous, but Job has proven from observation that this is false. Eliphaz cannot handle the truth, so he shouts louder. After all, there is no need to confuse the issue with facts.

A preacher once wrote in the margin of his sermon, "Point weak, pound the pulpit." Sometimes, people shout to cover their own confusion. When people "protest too much," it often means they are trying to convince themselves. When we are confident in our beliefs, we do not need to yell and scream. Truth spoken in a whisper is still truth.

Eliphaz is confused about Job's righteousness, but God is pleased by it. Remember how He bragged on Job in chapter one? God is pleased when His children walk in faith. Those faithful saints will one day judge the world. First Corinthians 6:1-2 promises, "Dare any of you, having a matter against another, go to law before the unjust, and not before the saints? Do ye not know that the saints shall judge the world? and if the world shall be judged by you, are ye unworthy to judge the smallest matters?"

Eliphaz was the founder "prosperity theology," which teaches that God blesses His children with over-abundance. Riches equal righteousness, and suffering equals sinfulness. We certainly can and should stand on the promises, but we are not God's boss. We should never assume that a wealthy person is godly and that a poor person is wicked.

For example, take the story Jesus told of the rich man and Lazarus. "There was a certain rich man . . . And there was a certain beggar named Lazarus . . . And it came to pass, that the beggar died, and was carried by the angels into Abraham's bosom: the rich man also died, and was buried; And in hell he lift up his eyes, being in torments" (Luke 16:19-23). The beggar went to Heaven, while the rich man went to Hell. Jesus told the story, so I believe it must be true!

CHAPTER SEVENTEEN
Job Succumbs to Grief

JOB'S ACCOUNT
JOB 23:1–24:25

"Eliphaz, I am hurting more than I can stand, and my grief weighs on me. I just cannot endure it anymore!

"I wish I knew where to find God—just to know how to approach His throne so that I could tell Him about my problems. If I could explain to Him what is happening, He would understand. He would strengthen me, deliver me from my false accusers, and ease my fears. I have searched for Him everywhere, but He is hidden. Oh, God, where are you?

"I know God sees me. He knows exactly where I am! I'm sure that God is not punishing me; He is only testing me. By the grace of God, I will pass this test!

"Eliphaz, I am still innocent, still following His commandments. God's words are more important than my daily food. God is still Sovereign, and I must accept what He sends my way. He does whatever He pleases, not what I want. I am afraid because I do not know what to expect from Him next. When I think of the things He has already done to me, my heart faints. He refused to kill me before all my struggles began, and He will not deliver me from them now.

"I wonder why God does not punish the wicked like you think He does. Certainly, He sees everything they do. Why does He allow them to live? They defraud by taking away the old landmarks and by stealing their neighbors' flocks. They take advantage of orphans and widows and refuse help to the poor and needy. Yet they prosper. Their children never go hungry. They ignore the naked shivering in the cold. They tear families apart and oppress the poor. They force their employees to work without so much as a drink of water. Still, God allows it to continue and refuses to punish the wicked.

"I do not understand how the wicked can be so blessed while I suffer so. There are sinners who rebel against the light of God and refuse to walk in the paths of righteousness. They wait for darkness to murder, steal, and commit adultery. Morning is a curse because it brings light; and if they are caught, they will be punished.

"But unknowingly, the wicked are rushing to judgment. They are about to reap the harvest of their evil ways. They will die just like everyone else and be forgotten. Though the wicked are exalted for a little while, they will soon be judged. I have told you the truth. Go ahead and try to prove I am lying."

Commentary

Job is looking for God and cannot find Him. How blessed you and I are on this side of the cross: Jesus has shown us the Father and provided access to Him. Jesus said to Philip, "He that hath seen me hath seen the Father" (John 14:9). The apostle Paul assures the saints at Ephesus:

> But now in Christ Jesus ye who sometimes were far off are made nigh by the blood of Christ. For he is our peace, who hath made both one, and hath broken down the middle wall of partition between us; Having abolished in his flesh the enmity, even the law of commandments contained in ordinances; for to make in himself of twain one new man, so making peace; And that he

might reconcile both unto God in one body by the cross, having slain the enmity thereby: And came and preached peace to you which were afar off, and to them that were nigh. For through him we both have access by one Spirit unto the Father. Now therefore ye are no more strangers and foreigners, but fellowcitizens with the saints, and of the household of God (Eph. 2:13-19).

When Jesus cried from the cross, "It is finished" (John 19:30); the veil in the temple at Jerusalem was torn in two from the top to the bottom, giving access to the presence of the Father. The torn veil symbolizes the broken body of Jesus. "Having therefore, brethren, boldness to enter into the holiest by the blood of Jesus, By a new and living way, which he hath consecrated for us, through the veil, that is to say, his flesh; And having an high priest over the house of God; Let us draw near with a true heart in full assurance of faith" (Heb. 10:19-22). Thanks be to God that we have access to God through the shed blood and broken body of our Lord Jesus Christ!

But even before the cross, God revealed Himself. There on the ash heap, when God seemed so far away and the criticism of his friends was so intense that he felt he could take no more, Job suddenly had a vision of God through the eyes of faith. God showed Himself for a moment, just when Job needed Him most. God opened Job's eyes to see what we saw in the first chapter—that this is not a punishment from God but rather a testing.

There is an important difference. Satan tempts us to bring out our worst, but God tests us to bring out our best. The testing of God is not punishment. Punishment tears down, while testing builds up. May God give us discernment to be able to tell the difference.

But the difference in punishment and testing for Job was that he was not guilty. He was still innocent, and that was very important to him. He was beginning to wonder about himself after the severe criticism of his friends. He was starting to believe that perhaps he had sinned and that God was angry with him. What a revelation to know that instead of being angry with him,

God was proud of him and loved him enough to put him through a time of testing for his betterment.

The apostle Peter knew about testing and wanted to encourage other believers who might go through similar circumstances. "Wherein ye greatly rejoice, though now for a season, if need be, ye are in heaviness through manifold temptations: That the trial of your faith, being much more precious than of gold that perisheth, though it be tried with fire, might be found unto praise and honour and glory at the appearing of Jesus Christ" (I Peter 1:6-7).

"Beloved, think it not strange concerning the fiery trial which is to try you, as though some strange thing happened unto you: But rejoice, inasmuch as ye are partakers of Christ's suffering; that, when his glory shall be revealed, ye may be glad also with exceeding joy" (I Peter 4:12-13). No testing seems joyous at the time, but it will be well worth every struggle and every heartache when we stand before Jesus and are able to offer Him our faith which has been tested by the fire.

Much of the support for Job's faith during the hard times was the Word of God. Job reveals his utmost dependence on the Word, saying that it is more important than his daily food. You and I need to meditate on the Word of God, hide it away in our hearts, and make it part of our daily lives. Surely, we, too, would find unknown strength through the hard times.

Psalm 1:2-3 says, "But his delight is in the law of the LORD; and in his law doth he meditate day and night. And he shall be like a tree planted by the rivers of water, that bringeth forth his fruit in his season; his leaf also shall not wither; and whatsoever he doeth shall prosper." Psalm 119:11 also emphasizes our need for God's Word: "Thy word have I hid in mine heart, that I might not sin against thee."

The Israelites were encouraged to meditate on God's Word as well. "This book of the law shall not depart out of thy mouth; but thou shalt meditate therein day and night, that thou mayest observe to do according to all that is written therein: for then thou shalt make thy way prosperous, and then thou shalt have good success" (Josh. 1:8). We are guaranteed success if we live according to the principles of God's Word—not success as measured by the world but success in the things of God.

Another support for Job's faith was his belief in the Sovereignty of God. God can and will do exactly as He pleases, and all things are under His control. Whatever you are going through right now has the permission, if not the blessing, of our great God and Father. Be faithful to God because He loves and cares for you as His own child!

One thing which troubled both Job and the prophet Habakkuk, along with a multitude of others (probably including you), was the fact that God allows the wicked to prosper. The psalmist lamented this fact:

> For I was envious at the foolish, when I saw the prosperity of the wicked . . . They are not in trouble as other men; neither are they plagued like other men . . . Behold, these are the ungodly, who prosper in the world; they increase in riches . . . When I thought to know this, it was too painful for me; Until I went into the sanctuary of God; then understood I their end. Surely thou didst set them in slippery places: thou castedst them down into destruction" (Psalm 73:3, 5, 12, 16-18).

When you feel the same way as David, just remember, this life is the only Heaven the wicked will ever know. And this life is the only Hell the saint will ever know. Do not begrudge the wicked of his happiness and pleasure—it is all he will ever get. Do not get too depressed during your times of suffering—it will all end one day when we get home.

CHAPTER EIGHTEEN
You Can Never Be Clean

BILDAD'S ACCOUNT
JOB 25:1-6

"God is always right. He controls men by dominion and fear. The numberless armies of the Lord march forth in an awesome display of power, making men afraid to disobey Him. Conversely, God rewards those who worship Him by shining the light of His goodness upon them. Godly men are encouraged to continue in their loyalty to God in order to receive His blessings. Men are merely puppets, reacting to their expectation of God, Who is everywhere and sees everything. Mere mortals can never be justified before God. We are unclean maggots in His sight. Compared to the glory of God, even the bright shining of the stars and the moon seems dull."

Commentary

This is a very short speech from Bildad. He thinks that men serve God for one of two reasons: fear or greed. They are either afraid of the punishments of God, or they are greedy for the blessings of God. They are either trying to escape Hell or hoping for a ticket to Heaven. I sincerely hope that there is another reason why people serve God—simply because they love Him.

Bildad says that no man can be justified in the sight of God—and perhaps he was right for his time—but on this side of the cross, men are justified by the shed blood of the Lord Jesus. Romans 3:24-26 tells us:

> Being justified freely by his grace through the redemption that is in Christ Jesus: Whom God hath set forth to be a propitiation through faith in his blood, to declare his righteousness for the remission of sins that are past, through the forbearance of God; To declare, I say, at this time his righteousness: that he might be just, and the justifier of him which believeth in Jesus.

Justification means to be made righteous in the sight of God and can only take place through the blood of Jesus. As a sinner and a keeper of the law, man could never be holy. Only the man whose sins have been washed clean in the blood of the Lamb can stand in the presence of God without guilt. That man can approach the Holy One because his record of sin has been purged.

CHAPTER NINETEEN
God Is Known through Nature

JOB'S ACCOUNT
JOB 26:1-14

"Bildad, stop and think for a moment. Has your arguing helped anyone, least of all me? Has your debating helped the powerless, saved the weak, or counseled the foolish? Have you said anything that is true? If you are trying to speak for God, perhaps you should learn something about Him.

"God created life out of nothing. His knowledge is so vast that even Hell and destruction cannot hide from Him. He hung the world on nothing, stretching the skies across the expanse of Heaven. He alone stores up water in the clouds to water the earth. You cannot see Him because He chooses to hide His throne behind a veil, but you can see the works of His hands. He keeps the oceans from flooding the earth. He establishes the hours of the day. He shoots thunderbolts as a display of His power. He sends mighty storms that stir up the seas. He brings down the proud. His hands placed the sun, moon, and stars in the heavens, and He is the Creator of all things.

"These are but a few of the mighty works of an all-powerful God. How little we really know about Him. How small in understanding are our puny, finite minds. Before the holy and righteous God, man becomes just a little speck of dust."

Commentary

After a very short speech by Bildad, we come to a very long speech by Job. Job's three friends seem to be getting weary; Zophar has already conceded. But while they are wearing down, Job is gaining strength. He has been in the presence of God through prayer. The revelations he received have lifted him up and poured strength into his physical body.

If you find yourself weary, run to the Father. Get alone with the Creator of the universe, allowing Him to undergird you with His strength. "As thy days, so shall thy strength be . . . The eternal God is thy refuge, and underneath are the everlasting arms" (Deut. 33:5, 27).

Job asks a very important question: "Who have you helped by all your talking?" Perhaps we should direct that same question to ourselves. We preach and pontificate. We talk until we are blue in the face, and it does no good. That stubborn and wayward child still will not listen or come to his senses. That estranged spouse still will not try to work out the problems. So, we talk, and talk, and talk some more, and keep on talking.

But maybe it is time to try another tactic: back off and give the other person space to come to a decision, talk to God, and correct your own faults. There are a number of things we can do when talking no longer does any good, but perhaps the most powerful one is to listen! Close your mouth and open your heart. How I wish one of these three friends would just get up, put his arms around Job, and say, "Hey, I'm listening."

In this section, Job displays considerable scientific knowledge. In an age when men understood little of the earth, Job knew about the vastness of space and about the earth hanging on nothing. He understood the process of evaporation, clouds, and rain. He marveled at the way God has decorated the heavens with the moon and stars and with clouds and blue sky. Who has not stood on the brink of night to watch God paint the evening with a sunset?

But Job realizes that God is the Creator of the spectacular and the common. A drop of rain and a speck of mud all come from the same God. How little we really understand about this great and mighty God we serve!

CHAPTER TWENTY
Job Proclaims His Innocence

JOB'S ACCOUNT
JOB 27:1-23

"I am still innocent! God has taken away my ability to judge the truth, and He continues to torment me. But as sure as God lives and gives me breath and as long as His Spirit is in me, I refuse to sin! I will not sin with my lips. I refuse to accept your condemnation. I hold fast to my righteousness, and I will not let it go. My conscience is clear, and I refuse to live in condemnation.

"My hope in God is strong, but what about the wicked who have no hope, those unrighteous men from whom God has withdrawn all hope? What will the wicked do when they finally realize that when they turned their back on God, He will no longer show them mercy?

"Bildad, let me teach you about God. The wicked will not prosper. His children will die by sword or by hunger. God will destroy him, and people will forget he ever existed. His own family will not mourn at his passing because they have seen God's anger upon him. His wealth will be divided among the innocent. His house will crumble like a spider's web. His nights will be filled with terror until God carries him away. His neighbors will rejoice that a wicked man has been removed from their presence."

Commentary

A clean conscience is a powerful thing. For a man to be able to stand up and say with a pure heart, "I have not sinned," is a blessing without comparison. "For if our heart condemn us, God is greater than our heart, and knoweth all things. Beloved, if our heart condemn us not, then have we confidence toward God" (I John 3:20-21). Acts 23:1 says, "And Paul, earnestly beholding the council, said, Men and brethren, I have lived in all good conscience before God until this day." And in the next chapter in Acts, we read, "And herein do I exercise myself, to have always a conscience void to offence toward God, and toward men" (Acts 24:16). Let us also strive to always maintain a clear conscience.

Job also said in this section, "Let me tell you about God." For a man who was having trouble finding God earlier, this is a remarkable turn-around. This should be the mission statement of every Christian: I will tell everyone I can about God.

CHAPTER TWENTY-ONE
Job Continues His Lesson About God

JOB'S ACCOUNT
JOB 28:1-28

"Look at some of the wonderful things God has created in the earth—silver, gold, iron, brass—all mined from the ground. God brings an end to the nighttime every morning with the rising of the sun. He releases the flood waters and dries them up again. The surface of the earth produces food for our sustenance, while the center of the earth is a flame of fire. So many precious things like gold and sapphire come from the earth!

"But there is something greater than gems and precious metals in the earth, things which even the birds or other creatures know. Wisdom and understanding are the treasures for which we should search. Wisdom is priceless, far more valuable than coral, pearls, rubies, topaz, or pure gold. Wisdom is the most valuable commodity on the market. Where can we find wisdom? Only God knows the road to wisdom. God saw wisdom, declared that it was good for man, prepared the heart of man to seek after wisdom, and searched out all wisdom so He could reveal it to His children."

Commentary

Job is describing the wisdom of God. Can you imagine what would happen to the rotation of the earth if the weight of the water in the Atlantic

Ocean over-balanced the weight of the water in the Pacific Ocean? This world would wobble through space like a tire out of balance. I am glad there is a wise God in control. He still teaches clouds how to rain. He still shows the thunder how to light up the sky with lightning. What a wise God He is!

But you can be wise, too. In just two easy steps, you can go from stupid, ignorant, and unlearned to brilliant. Listen carefully.

STEP #1: Fear the Lord.

The smartest thing a person can do is fall on their face in awe and reverence before a holy God. Only when a person recognizes the awesome power of God can he really begin to be wise. "The fear of the LORD is the beginning of wisdom: and the knowledge of the holy is understanding" (Prov. 9:10). When you fear God with all your heart, you have nothing else to fear. "There is no fear in love; but perfect love casteth out fear: because fear hath torment. He that feareth is not made perfect in love. We love him, because he first loved us" (I John 4:18-19).

STEP #2: Depart from evil.

If you give reverence to the Lord, you will want to please Him in all things. You will want to avoid everything that remotely brings dishonor to His name. "The fear of the LORD is to hate evil: pride, and arrogancy, and the evil way, and the froward mouth, do I hate" (Prov. 8:13). "Abstain from all appearance of evil" (I Thess. 5:22). Second Timothy 2:21-22 says, "If a man therefore purge himself from these, he shall be a vessel unto honour, sanctified, and meet for the master's use, and prepared unto every good work. Flee also youthful lusts: but follow righteousness, faith, charity, peace, with them that call on the Lord out of a pure heart."

CHAPTER TWENTY-TWO
Job Reminisces About the Past

JOB'S ACCOUNT
JOB 29:1–30:1-31

"How I wish I could go back to the days when God preserved me, when His light shone upon me, and when there were no dark paths to walk. In my younger days, I understood the secrets of God; the Almighty surrounded me while my children played at my feet. I was prosperous. I was respected. I served as a judge in the gate of the city; so young men moved out of my way; and old men stood up in respect at my presence. Everyone listened to me—even princes and noblemen—and everyone blessed me.

"Because I had been blessed, I tried to bless others. I delivered food to the poor and fatherless and helped those who could not help themselves. I stood up for the oppressed, while opposing the wicked.

"I was prosperous and content. I thought I would die in my own home surrounded by my family after a very long and healthy life. I was young and strong. I imagined that I would remain a young warrior with a strong bow in my hand. Men listened attentively to my advice. My words were like showers of rain on a dry field. My approval made their faces light up with joy. I was their chief advisor.

"Ah, but those were the good, old days. Young men mock me. Their fathers are worth less than my sheepdogs—foolish, base, and vile men. The gang of ruffians have to scramble for a bite of bread; they live like outlaws in caves; they bray like wild donkeys, but they mock *me*. They sing songs about me. I am their new joke. They hate me and spit in my face. They trip me when I walk and play tricks on me. They have lost all restraint, crushing me on every side.

"Their disrespect has broken my spirit. My bones are pierced with stabbing pain, and my aching muscles have no rest. My boils have ruptured, staining my clothes and making them stick to my body. The stench is overpowering.

"Oh, God, You have cast me into the mud where I became no more than dust among the ashes. I pray, but You refuse to listen. You are not paying any attention to me. Your strong hand persecutes me. You are going to kill me, but You prolong the agony. You are killing me slowly, though I cry for release.

"Oh, God, I do not deserve this! I weep when others are in trouble, and my soul grieves for the poor. But when I looked for good to happen to me, evil came. When I waited for light, darkness came. My insides are in utter turmoil because of these afflictions which have overcome me."

Commentary

Sometimes, we need to remember the past. Sometimes, those old memories keep us going. In times of trouble, it is good to remember God's past faithfulness. In times of sorrow, it is good to remember God's past comfort. Sitting on the ash heap, Job remembers how everything was before his affliction. But Job is singing "Amazing Grace" in reverse. His version of the song goes like this: "I once was found, but now I'm lost. I once could see, but now I'm blind."

Everything used to be good for Job. But now, children mock him; he is afflicted; God seems cruel to him; and he feels that he does not deserve the things that have happened to him. One of his greatest sorrows comes to light in the passage where he accuses God of dissolving all his substance with the wind. It was a strong wind that blew down the house where his children were having their party, killing them. You can feel the agony of a parent's heartbreak for the loss of his children. The loss of all his material things seems to have little effect on Job, but he can hardly bear the grief caused by the death of his children.

Thinking about the death of his children immediately suggests his own death and how he wishes he could die, too. He almost seems to border on blasphemy as he accuses God of killing him slowly instead of quickly. But if we look closely, we realize that grief really is a slow killer and probably one of the hardest things in the world to deal with effectively. I certainly cannot condemn. Although I have never lost a child, I can stretch my imagination and feel just a little of what it must be like for a parent to out-live a child.

But Job rallies again as his mind turns back to God. Watch him as he re-affirms his integrity.

CHAPTER TWENTY-THREE
Job Takes Steps in Guaranteed Holiness

JOB'S ACCOUNT
JOB 31:1-40

"My life has been beyond reproach. As a young man, I made a covenant with my eyes to remain sexually pure. I am determined not to look upon anything which will tempt me to sin because God destroys the wicked and punishes the sinner. God sees all my actions and counts all my steps. Surely, He will not hold me guiltless if I sin in this matter.

"As an additional safeguard, I am asking you, my friends, to hold me accountable for my actions. If I have walked in sin, then judge me justly. If I am guilty, then let me bear my punishment. If I am guilty of sexual impurity or of any ulterior motives, then let my wife be another man's servant and let her become a harlot. Sexual sin is a heinous crime, an iniquity deserving of punishment. Lust is a fire that consumes everything in its path until everything is destroyed and all a man's profit is eaten up.

"If I have mistreated my servants, how will I stand before God as His servant? What would I say to God when He came to question me on their behalf? The same God created both me and my servant so that we are equals.

"If I have withheld any comfort from the poor, the widow, the orphan, the naked, or the helpless, then let my arm fall off. I would rather receive punishment from men for my sins than to be punished by God. Destruction from God terrifies me, and I faint when I consider His majesty.

"If I have trusted in riches, worshipped the sun or the moon, been seduced by bribes, or dealt deceitfully with others, then I would be guilty of denying God and would deserve to be punished. If I have rejoiced in the misfortunes of my enemies or become proud when my enemy suffers the consequences of his sin, then I deserve punishment. I should be brought down if I have cursed anyone or failed to meet the needs of my own household or helped strangers in need. If I have tried to cover my sins or if I have feared men instead of obeying God, then I deserve my punishment.

"Will someone listen to me? Oh, God, please answer me! I wish my enemies had written their accusations down in a book. In fact, I dare you to put it in writing, so everyone can see my accusations listed. Just tell me what I am guilty of so that I can repent publicly and before God. Since no accusations are forthcoming, I rest my case."

Commentary

How refreshing to see a man honest with his weaknesses while being totally committed to overcoming them. Surely, more men have fallen over sexual sins than any other sin. Just check the list: Samson, David, Solomon, the men of Israel with the women of Moab—not to mention some well-known names within the Christian community of our generation. Although our society makes light of our old-fashioned ideas about sex and marriage, God is still very committed to the truth of His Word.

Two of the Ten Commandments deal with the issue of sexual purity. "Thou shalt not commit adultery . . . thou shalt not covet thy neighbour's wife" (Exod. 20:14, 17). From the very beginning, God's plan has been one man for one woman for one lifetime. "Therefore shall a man leave his father and his mother, and shall cleave unto his wife: and they shall be one flesh" (Gen. 2:24). Jesus, quoting this text, added, "Wherefore they are no more twain, but one flesh. What therefore God hath joined together, let not man put asunder" (Matt. 19:6). Because the marriage vows are sacred in the sight of God, men must withstand both the temptations within and without marriage. God does not take lightly anyone breaking the vows of marriage; and in a society where half of all marriages end in divorce, there will be a lot of questions to answer when we stand before a holy God.

Christian men should make their marriage a priority. They should guard their sexual purity with determination and strength. This goes a lot deeper than actually cheating on your wife. Jesus included a section about sexual purity in His Sermon on the Mount. "Ye have heard that it was said by them of old time, Thou shalt not commit adultery: But I say unto you, That whosoever looketh on a woman to lust after her hath committed adultery with her already in his heart" (Matt. 5:27-28). You see, it starts in the heart and in the mind long before it is acted out physically.

So, men, keep your heart and your mind pure. Make a covenant with your eyes not to look at anything, other than your wife, which would cause you to lust. Turn off the television if necessary. Throw away the magazines. Find other topics of discussion when you are around "the guys." God will honor your commitment to His Word.

Another good thing Job did was to ask his friends to hold him accountable for his actions. You need someone who will love you enough to call your hand when you make bad decisions or fall into temptation. There needs to be at least one other person in your life to whom you can confide your weaknesses and to whom you are accountable for your actions. This person needs to be able to ask you, "What movies did you watch while you were away on this last business trip? Did you compromise in any way your marriage and your relationship with your wife?" Knowing that you have a friend to hold you accountable will go a long way when you are under attack from the enemy.

Job is a brave man to ask for a public accounting. He stands before the world and says, in effect, "If anybody has any evidence that I have sinned, let them bring it forth." That is a man who is sure about himself. Apparently, no one came forth with a public accusation (not even his three friends), so Job rests his case.

CHAPTER TWENTY-FOUR
Elihu Speaks

ELIHU'S ACCOUNT
JOB 32:1–33:33

"I hesitate to express my opinion because I am young, and you are all very old men. I have always been taught that age should speak and that those of advanced years should be the ones to teach wisdom. It has always been a tradition that younger men respect their elders and that they speak only when spoken to. However, there is a spirit in man that forces me to act. It is the inspiration of God which gives understanding to men, regardless of their age.

"Great men are not always wise, and the elderly do not always perfectly understand judgment. Therefore, if you will listen to me, I will give my opinion. I waited for you to speak. I listened to you as you gave your argument, and I was silent as you considered what you were going to say. I have listened to this whole debate; and none of you has convinced Job that your arguments are sound. Not one of you has answered his questions. I am amazed (and a little disappointed) that none of you aged men have discovered wisdom. For all your talk and for all your claims of superior knowledge, the only thing you could come up with is, 'God, and not man, has done this to Job.'

"Now, I realize that Job has not been talking to me, and I certainly cannot answer him with the kind of speeches you have used. But everyone seems to be finished. You are all sitting here with your mouth open in amazement, and no one is talking. I have kept silent, waiting to make sure that you were finished. I have listened to all sides of this debate carefully; and now, I will assume that you are finished and will give you my opinion. I am just bursting at the seams to share my opinion. I need to get this off my chest.

"I am not here to take sides in this debate. It is not my purpose to say things just to impress you. I understand that if flattery were my motive, my Maker would quickly destroy me.

"Job, please allow me to speak out of the uprightness of my heart. Please listen to me, and I will speak in a way that you can clearly understand. The Spirit of God has made me, and the breath of the Almighty has given me life. Job, if you can answer me or if you can prove my words wrong, please stand up. I am willing to give you the floor at any time.

"You wished for someone to come in God's behalf to answer your questions; and behold, here I am. But I am just a man like you, so you will not be afraid when I speak terrible things. I will not try to scare you to death or use heavy-handed measures to convince you that I am right. I have listened to you, and this is a summary of what I think you said. You believe you are innocent but that God is against you and counts you as His enemy.

"Job, you are not fair in blaming God. God is greater than man. You can fight against Him all you want, but He will win. He is not under any obligation to give account of Himself to you. But even though God is not required to speak, He chooses to do so. He speaks to us in dreams or through visions. While we sleep, God opens our ears to give us instruction. Then in the waking hours, He withdraws Himself to keep men from being lifted up in pride.

"God also speaks to man through life experiences. The very fact that you are still living is because He has allowed it. If God were not still speaking to His people, you would be dead now. God also speaks through pain. He chastens a man upon a sick bed so that his bones ache with severe pain. God takes away a man's appetite so that the sight of bread or delicious food turns his stomach. His body wastes away to nothing so that his bones stick out like a skeleton. It is God speaking when a man draws near to the grave and when his life is in danger. God is speaking through dreams and visions, through prolonging your life, through your suffering and pain, through your loss of appetite, through the frailty of your body, and through the dangers you have faced. Job, God is speaking to you through all these things—if you would just listen to Him.

"Unfortunately, we can understand the voice of God only through a mediator. There must be a messenger and someone to interpret that message. That only happens perhaps one time in a thousand. Very rarely is there someone sent from God to reveal to a man that he is righteous. But when the message comes, it brings the gracious news that a ransom has been found. When God has found that person to pay the ransom price, everything changes for the better for the person who was afflicted. He will pray to God, and God will be favorable unto his prayer. That man will be able to look upon the face of God with great rejoicing, and God will impart to him righteousness.

"Right now, God is looking down on us. If any will confess his sins and admit that he has perverted that which was right, God will hear that man's confession. He will deliver his soul from Hell and will extend his life on this earth. This is the way God works with men to rescue them from Hell and to teach them wisdom while they are in the land of the living.

"Oh, Job, please pay attention to me. Be quiet and let me speak. If you have any questions, I will try to answer them, for I really want to justify you. If not, just listen to me and let me teach you wisdom."

Commentary

After a very long speech by Job, there was silence. No one spoke. No one came forth to challenge Job's testimony. After three rounds of debate, Eliphaz, Bildad, and Zophar had exhausted all their arguments and still had not proven that Job's problems were the result of sin. Job could not be shaken from his faith in God and from his conviction that he had done nothing wrong. Because Job was righteous in his own eyes, these three ceased to answer Job. When a person is convinced in his heart that he is innocent, that faith is hard to shake.

Now, as the silence grows longer and a bit uncomfortable, a new voice breaks the spell. It comes from the audience which had gathered from time to time listening to the debate between Job and his three friends. The young man who speaks now is named Elihu, the son of Barachel. The name Elihu means "my God is He," so it appears that he is a very religious person who loves and serves God. Perhaps he will have better answers that the other three. Perhaps he will speak some words of comfort and encouragement to Job. Elihu's father, Barachel, was from the family of Buz. From Genesis 22:21, we learn that Buz was the nephew of Abraham (son of Abraham's brother Nahor) and that he was the brother to Uz, who was a descendant of Job. So it seems that Elihu is a relative of Job and that they are both related to Abraham.

Listening to the debate, a spirit of anger began to build in Elihu. He began to be angry with Job because it seemed that he was trying to justify himself rather than God. It seemed more important for Job to be right than for God to be right. But he also got angry at the three friends of Job because they had not come up with an answer to Job's questions. Yet they had persisted in condemning him as a sinner without any real evidence.

Elihu is a young man with a lot of patience and respect for his elders. He has waited through this long debate for a turn to speak, but he would not interrupt because all the men were older than he. But when the silence grew longer and he saw that no one else was going to speak, he took the floor.

So far, I have been fairly impressed with Elihu. He has shown a lot of wisdom in dealing with disputes like the one between Job and his friends. It seems to me that there are five steps to follow. Perhaps we could call them "Elihu's Five Steps to Resolving Conflict":

STEP #1: Listen to all sides before making a judgment.

Elihu patiently sat through all this long debate just listening. While the others were intent only upon telling their side of the story and convincing someone else that their position was the correct one, Elihu just listened. It has been said that God gave us two ears and only one mouth, which proves that we should listen twice as much as we talk. James 1:19 admonishes, "Wherefore, my beloved brethren, let every man be swift to hear, slow to speak, slow to wrath." What a beautiful description: swift ears and a slow tongue. Before you can make a judgment call, you must listen not just to two sides but to all sides.

STEP #2: Be neutral.

Elihu does not take sides—he admits up front that he is angry with Job and with his friends. While that may not be the ideal start, at least he is not biased in one direction. Once we start taking sides, we lose objectivity. We can no longer see the whole picture, but we rather focus on trying to prove one point or another.

STEP #3: Be honest.

Do not resort to flattery. "For I know not to give flattering titles; in so doing my maker would soon take me away" (Job 32:22). Elihu has waited patiently because these men were older than he, but he does not allow that to keep him from ultimately saying what is on his mind. He bows to their seniority, but he does not try to flatter them. When we resort to flattery, our goal is to impress someone or to gain friends to our cause with silky words. May God give us the grace to speak honestly and to state our opinions without having to butter up others first. True compliments are great and should be shared often, but flattery is nothing more than subtle lying.

STEP #4: Come as an equal.

Elihu does not try to exalt himself like some of the others have done. He is just a man like everyone else. Sometimes, when we pontificate and try to lord it over others, the only thing we succeed in doing is making enemies. We should always remember that everyone is equal in the sight of God.

STEP #5: Summarize what the other person is saying to be sure you heard correctly.

Elihu proceeds to tell Job what he thought he heard him say. This gives the other person an opportunity to correct your interpretation of his words. Sometimes, people hear what they think another person is saying and not necessarily what the person meant. If you can summarize what you think he said, there will be good groundwork laid for reconciliation.

Try these five steps next time you get into a conflict, and may they help resolve some of the problems you have with another person!

Elihu then tells Job that he is wrong to accuse God. God is Sovereign, and He does exactly as He pleases without asking our opinion. When will God's children learn to let their Father take care of His world?

Elihu says that God speaks to men through dreams and visions, through the very process of living, through pain, through loss of appetite, through frailty of body, and through dangers. God can—and does—speak to us through all of those means, but that does not necessarily mean that God is the One Who sends those difficulties. It does not mean that a person in pain has sinned, and God had to use that pain to get his attention. God has better ways of speaking than that.

Hebrews tells us, "God, who at sundry times and in divers manners spake in time past unto the fathers by the prophets, Hath in these last days spoken unto us by his Son" (Heb. 1:1-2). "He that hath an ear, let him hear what the Spirit saith unto the churches" (Rev. 2:7). May God give us spiritual ears to hear the voice of God and to respond to the slightest hint of a whisper from His Holy Spirit.

Next, Elihu gives a powerful revelation about the work of our Lord Jesus Christ. He told Job that we could only understand God through an interpreter. How true that is! We need someone who speaks the language! When God spoke with an audible voice from Mount Sinai, the children of Israel were so frightened that they requested that God not speak to them directly any more. "And all the people saw the thunderings, and the lightnings, and the noise of the trumpet, and the mountain smoking: and when the people saw it, they removed, and stood afar off. And they said unto Moses, Speak thou with us, and we will hear: but let not God speak with us, lest we die" (Exod. 20:18-19).

They were so scared of the display of God's majesty that they were afraid they were going to die. But Jesus came to interpret God for us. He is the Word of God made flesh. John confirms this for us when he writes, "In the beginning was the Word, and the Word was with God, and the Word was God. And the Word was made flesh, and dwelt among us, (and we beheld his glory, the glory as of the only begotten of the Father,) full of grace and truth" (John 1:1, 14). Jesus is the revealed Word of God to this earth, and we can understand the Father through the Word.

Once an interpreter arrives, God says, "Deliver him from going down to the pit: I have found a ransom" (Job 33:24). The same One Who comes as the Interpreter has also paid the ransom price for the redemption of the soul. Men who were held in captivity to sin can now go free. The blood of Jesus paid the price to set every captive free from the bondage of sin once and for all!

Even though he speaks more truth than the other friends of Job, Elihu is somewhat arrogant. "I am here in the place of God. I am here to teach you wisdom." Well, he is a young man with a lot of zeal, so let us see how good a job he does in teaching Wisdom 101.

CHAPTER TWENTY-FIVE
Job, You Are Wrong

ELIHU'S ACCOUNT
JOB 34:1-35:16

"Listen to me, all you wise men. Job has made a mistake! We can agree among ourselves about the validity of his speeches. Job lied when he claimed to be righteous in the sight of God! He was mistaken in thinking that his wounds came about without any wrongdoing on his part. Why, look at him! He actually enjoys being reproached because it makes him feel more righteous.

"Let me set the record straight—God judges righteously! God cannot commit evil, but He will judge every sinner. No one elected God for His position. No one trained Him to do His job. Man did not invent God and set Him as Controller of the earth. God is in that position because He is God, and no one else can tell Him how to run things. If God ever withdraws His breath, every living thing will perish; and men will return to the dust.

"Just because you hate good government, would you dare accuse the king of wickedness? To condemn the innocent, is it proper to say to the prince, 'You are ungodly?' Of course not! If you then would not be so presumptuous before earthly rulers, how much less before the One Who is not impressed by princes or the One Who regards the rich and the poor alike because they all belong to Him? They are His creation, the work of His hands, and something He made from the dust of the earth. They will all die in a moment!

"God sees everything, so there is no way to hide your wickedness from his eyes. God judges correctly. He has not punished Job more than he deserves. God breaks mighty men in little pieces and promotes other men to their position. He overturns evil works and openly punishes wicked men for turning away from Him and for not listening to His counsel. God has heard the cry of the poor and afflicted and has pronounced judgment on the wicked.

"Once God has spoken, His decree is unchangeable. When God hides His face, who can find Him? Otherwise, hypocrites would reign, and all the people would be ensnared by evil. God is Sovereign, and He does as He pleases. The only recourse we have before God is repentance of our sins and a decision to live for Him instead of living in sin. What you want does not matter at all to God. His plan will be carried out regardless of your thoughts on the situation. Everything will be done according to the will of God.

"Now, listen to me. Job is guilty because he simply does not know what he is talking about. He answers questions like a wicked man, so let's keep on cross-examining him to the finish! He is rebellious and refuses to listen to the reason of his friends. He claps his hands while we are trying to talk and does not give us time to finish our debate. He simply talks too much!

"Job, what you need to do is to seek after God. Do you think you are correct in saying that you are more righteous than God? You wonder if being cleansed from your sin will be any profit to you. Well, let me tell you and your three friends something. God is so much higher than you are that He is not injured by your sins, even though they be multiplied. If you were the most righteous man in the world, your righteousness would not profit God. Your wickedness will hurt you and perhaps oppress multitudes of others. Your righteousness will bless you, but God is still God regardless of anything you do.

"Job, what you need to do is call upon God. Recognize Him as the Creator Who spoke everything into existence in the beginning. Recognize Him also as the God of the present Who gives us songs in the night and Who teaches us and makes us wise.

"God refuses to answer your prayers because you are full of pride. He does not pay any attention to you because of your vanity. Even though you cannot see God, you can rest assured that He will judge righteously. That is the problem now. You would not trust God, and He has visited you in His anger. He has brought all these calamities upon you because of your sin."

Commentary

What a disappointment! After such a good start, Elihu now sounds just like the other three. He sounds like the old adage, "Sin produces suffering, and righteousness produces blessing. If you are suffering, it is proof that you have sinned. Prosperity is proof of your righteousness." Somehow, Job just cannot get away from that theme. What is even sadder is that diabolical theme is still around. Even knowing the truth from the Word of God, people still judge others on the basis of what they own or what they are going through.

But Elihu polishes some great sparkling gemstones in this passage. For instance, how blessed we are to understand that we are the handiwork of a powerful God. He made us from the dust of the earth and breathed His life into our nostrils. Because He created us, He knows all about us. He knows how to minister to us when we are hurting, how to encourage us when we are discouraged, and how to bless us through the rough places. He knows exactly what we need because He made us.

Thanks be to God that He walks in the night when the heartaches and problems are the worst. He is there in the deepest valley of despair, even the valley of death. His presence draws close to us when our strength is almost gone, and He undergirds us with His everlasting arms.

Paul and Silas had been beaten and put in the jail in Philippi for preaching about Jesus. They were in the maximum security part of the jail, their feet in stocks, their backs bruised and bleeding, and their spirits disappointed. Surely, this is about as bad as it gets. But all of a sudden, the presence of a God Who gives songs in the night came into that jail cell. "And at midnight Paul and Silas prayed, and sang praises unto God: and the prisoners heard them. And suddenly there was a great earthquake, so that the foundations of the prison were shaken: and immediately all the doors were opened, and every one's bands were loosed" (Acts 16:25-26). God's presence brought songs in the night in spite of everything they were going through.

Job is a night-singer, too. During some of the most trying times of his life, he has had a revelation of God and burst out into song:

- "The LORD gave, and the LORD hath taken away; blessed be the name of the LORD" (1:21).
- "Though he slay me, yet will I trust in him" (13:15).
- "For I know that my redeemer liveth, and that he shall stand at the latter day upon the earth" (19:25).
- "When he hath tried me, I shall come forth as gold" (23:10).

What beautiful songs to sing in the middle of the night when darkness is all around us and all hope seems gone. Those songs which remind us of Jesus and what He has done for us will lift our spirits and encourage our faith to keep holding on to God until morning comes.

You, too, can be a night-singer if you will remember Who God is. When life is at its worst, you can still look up to God and praise Him because He is God. That long night of pain, suffering, and heartache will be a bit better when we learn to sing songs in the night.

CHAPTER TWENTY-SIX
I Have Perfect Knowledge

ELIHU'S ACCOUNT
JOB 36:1–37:24

"Job, be patient with me just a little longer while I prove to you that I speak on God's behalf. Because of my far-reaching knowledge, I only ascribe righteousness to God. My words are true because I have perfect knowledge.

"Out of my perfect knowledge, let me share with you some of God's attributes. Behold, God is mighty and loves everyone. He punishes the wicked, cares for the poor, and provides for the righteous by putting them on the throne with kings and by establishing them and exalting them forever. He reveals to those who are in bondage which sins have caused their imprisonment. He opens their ears to hear His discipline and commands them to turn from sin. If they obey and serve Him, they will spend their days in prosperity and their years in pleasure. But if they disobey, they will die without knowledge.

"Job, God delivers the poor, and He would have delivered you, too, if you had repented. He would have rescued you out of the tight place and set you in wide, open spaces. He would have spread your table with an abundance of delicious food. But you have refused God's help; therefore, you are reaping the judgment of the wicked. God's justice has finally caught up with you. God is angry enough to wipe you out with a single stroke. There is not enough ransom money in the world to deliver you from God's wrath. He will cut you off in the darkness of night when you least expect it. Job, you had better wake up! Turn away from your sin before it is too late!

"Oh, Job. God is so great! He is a Teacher like no other, and He is above sin. We should praise Him so that others may see His glory. God's ways are beyond our finding out; neither can we know the number of His years. We see His handiwork in every drop of rain that falls from the clouds, but who can understand the process by which those raindrops gather in the clouds to be poured out upon us? Or who can understand God's presence in the tabernacle where He speaks with men? Who can understand sunlight, which God spreads over the earth and has the power to penetrate to the bottom of the sea? These are things beyond the comprehension of men but things which God uses to either bless or punish. The same clouds which pour out the rain needed for abundant crops also block out the sunlight to make the earth dark. All these things are in the hands of God.

"When I think of the awesome power of God, my heart trembles so violently that it moves out of its place. Listen carefully to the sound of the thunder going out of the mouth of God. He directs the lightning flashes to the ends of the earth. We cannot comprehend the great things that proceed from His voice. God tells the snow, spring showers, and thunderstorms when to make their appearance. He tells the beasts when to stay in their dens, so they will be protected from the coming weather. He sends the whirlwind out of the south and cold out of the north. By the breath of God, frost is given, and the surfaces of the lakes are frozen.

"Listen to this, Job. Stand still and consider the wonderful works of God. Do you know when God scattered the clouds and allowed the sun to shine? Do you know how God balances the clouds in the sky? This is the work of One Who is perfect in knowledge! God is more awesome in His majesty than we can understand. He is excellent in power, judgment, justice, and mercy. We stand in holy reverence of Him, but He is not at all impressed with us."

Commentary

Elihu goes from polite to arrogant to pompous in the blink of an eye. How far the young man has fallen! But when he gets his eyes off himself long enough to look at God, he makes some powerful statements about the majesty and grandeur of God.

God is great! God is mighty in power! He is a Teacher like no other. Thunder is the roar of God's voice; indeed, God controls all of nature, sending the wind, the rain, and the sunshine and even tells the animals when it is time to hibernate for the winter. God is perfect in knowledge! He even knows how to balance the clouds in the sky so that they float on a breeze and drift lazily across the heavens. What a great God we serve!

In fact, now that we have heard a lot of opinions from man, God finally steps in to show His purpose and plan in Job's life.

CHAPTER TWENTY-SEVEN
God's Questions

GOD'S ACCOUNT
JOB 38:1-40:2

"Job, you and your friends have been talking foolishly because you do not have all the facts. You simply do not know what you are talking about. Be a man. The childish arguments are over. This is going to be serious business for mature men. I am going to give you a quiz in which I will ask the questions, and you will give the answers.

"First of all, where were you when I laid the foundation of the earth? Tell me if you understand the answer. Who set up the specifications for the earth? Who surveyed its dimensions and measurements? What are the foundations of the earth fastened to? Who laid the cornerstone of the world in place in order for construction to begin? Who was present on that day to hear the morning stars singing together and all the angels shouting for joy? Were you there that day, Job?

"Second, Who set the boundaries for the sea? On the day the seas first burst into waves, Who set up restrictions so that they could only go so far? Who clothed the sea with clouds and wrapped the depths in a swaddling band of thick darkness? Who separated the waters of the earth into their proper places and set boundaries for the waves of the seas so that they can come only so far and no further?

"Have you commanded the morning, or did you teach the dawn to know its place? Morning spreads across the earth from one end to the other, shaking the wicked from their evil deeds, which require the cover of darkness.

"Job, can you find the springs of water which feed the seas or measure the depth of the sea? Rivers and streams run continuously into the sea from springs often hidden in a mountain ridge. The depth of the sea has never been explored.

"Have you seen through the gates of death to see what is on the other side? Do you understand how big the earth is? Job, do you know where light and darkness live? Can you determine where they end? Can you find the paths which lead to their homes? Do you know the answers because you were born when all these things were taking place? Or have you learned the answers during your long life?

"Do you understand the treasures of snow or hail? Do you know that I have reserved these two? These are weapons which I use in the day of battle.

"Does light separate for the wind to blow through? How does the wind blow through light without blowing it away? Who prepared a water-course for excess rain water to drain off? Rain falls, even where there are no people. It soaks the dry ground and causes the plants to bud. Who made a path for the lightning? When static electricity builds up it creates a bolt of lightning and a powerful boom. Who is the Father of the rain or the dewdrops?

"Did you give birth to the ice and the frost? They freeze solid the tops of the waters as if one had rolled a stone on top of them.

"What about constellations? Can you bind the planets or control the solar system? Can you bring about the seasons? Do you know all the laws by which the heavens are ruled? Can you establish the laws of the earth and enforce them? Can you command the clouds to produce rain? Do the lightning bolts report to you?

"Who put wisdom and understanding in the heart of man? Who is intelligent enough to number the clouds? Who can withhold the rains so that the earth becomes dry and thirsty?

"What about the wild animals? Can you hunt food for the lion and his cubs? Do you provide for the raven when his young ones cry out for lack of food? Do you understand the birthing cycle of the wild animals? Can you predict when they will give birth? Do you know how long their gestation period is? All the animals give birth to offspring after their own likeness. They are born with the ability to eat and grow and to perpetuate the cycle.

"Job, Who set the wild donkey free? He lives in the barren wilderness. He does not submit to a driver or master. The mountain range is his pasture as he searches for his food.

"Can you tame the wild ox? Will he be willing to work for you in return for his food? Can you bind him and force him to plow your fields? Will you trust his great strength to labor in your behalf? Do you trust him to harvest your crops and gather them into your barns?

"Did you create the peacock and the ostrich? Are you the one who gave beautiful feathers to the peacock? Did you create the ostrich with wings which cannot fly or give her such useless feathers? She lays her eggs in the sand and forgets that her foot might crush them or a wild beast might eat them. She has no more concern for her young than if they belonged to someone else. She labors in vain without a care in the world because God has deprived her of wisdom and withheld from her understanding. She lifts up her long neck and laughs at the horse and his rider knowing that they cannot outrun her.

"Did you give the horse his strength? Did you clothe his neck with thunder? Can you make him to be afraid? When he flares his nostrils, you can feel the awesome glory of his being. He paws anxiously in the valley; he rejoices in his strength as he prepares to meet the armed man in battle. He mocks fear, is not frightened, and will not run from the sword.

"Does the hawk fly by your wisdom? Did you train her to stretch out her wings toward the south? Does the eagle mount up at your command? Did you teach her to make her nest in the high places? She makes her home on the top of the rocks in a very secure place. From there, she searches for her prey.

Her keen eyesight enables her to detect the movement of her prey, which she catches to share with her little ones.

"Do you presume to instruct the Almighty? You who have been reproving God. Give an answer!"

Commentary

After a very long speech from Elihu, silence reigned again. Job had no response to the accusations Elihu hurled against him. Job's friends had nothing further to add. No one knew what to say. In the silence, God appeared! When everyone had exhausted all their knowledge and displayed all their expertise, God spoke. "Then the Lord answered Job out of the whirlwind" (Job 38:1).

The journey of faith has come to its ultimate goal—the manifestation of God Himself and the confirmation of the things which we believe. Hebrews 11:1 says, "Now faith is the substance of things hoped for, the evidence of things not seen." Those things which Job had hoped for have happened. Faith has paid off because God has come on the scene in a manifestation of Himself, and nothing else matters!

Will you allow me to make some observations before we continue?

1. Keep pressing on!

We have muddled through thirty-seven chapters of debate from five different people in order to get to this point. If you have not seen the manifestation of your faith yet, hold on and do not give up. Grab on tight, stand firm, and keep on going! Faith will be rewarded. Those who quit in the middle of the battle will never win the victory. Those who give up hope and lose faith during the testing will never see the manifestation of the glory of God. Whatever you do, do not miss seeing God when He makes Himself known. It may not be until we get home to glory; but if it takes that long, keep holding on to that nail-scarred hand. Keep your faith firmly in the Christ of Calvary. Never, never, never give up!

2. Be still and listen to God.

God does not enter the debate. He waits for everyone to wear themselves out, to voice all their opinions, and to present all their arguments. Only when they are all quiet does God speak. Perhaps if we would learn to be quite in His presence more often, God would speak sooner!

3. When God shows up, nothing else matters.

God does not answer one single question about why people suffer. In fact, He does not answer any questions; but in His presence, the questions are not important anymore. God has come, and that is enough.

4. God comes unexpectedly.

We miss God sometimes because we are not expecting the unexpected. Job was expecting God to come as a Judge with a verdict of "not guilty." Instead, God came in a whirlwind. I missed God. I read through chapter thirty-eight twice, and I missed Him. I, too, was looking for God to speak from Heaven in an audible voice. I was looking for thunder and lightning or maybe an earthquake. But the third time through, I saw God; and God was in the whirlwind! When you are dealing with God, learn to expect the unexpected. Look at some of the places God has appeared:

- In a bush which was burning and yet not consumed by the fire (Exod. 3:2)
- On a ladder where angels were walking up and down between Heaven and earth (Gen. 28:12).
- In a "still, small voice" after the wind and the earthquake were gone (I Kings 19:12).
- In a wheel in the middle of a wheel (Ezek. 1:16).
- In a sheet filled with supposedly unclean animals (Acts 10:11-15).
- In a trumpet blast (Exod. 19:19).

- In a manger in Bethlehem (Luke 2:7).
- To the disciples in the ship, who thought He was a ghost and almost let Him walk by (Mark 6:47-50).
- On the road to Emmaus (Luke 24:13-35).

May God open our eyes to see the gentle Galilean as He walks with us on the road of life. May we, too, learn to expect God in unexpected places.

God is the Creator! He drew up all the specifications, measured out all the dimensions, and hung the world on nothing. He is the Divine Architect Who drew up the blueprints and the Divine Builder Who constructed everything according to the specifications.

At creation, the morning stars burst into song; and you can still see them twinkling in time to the music of Heaven. All of creation joins in a mighty chorus of praise to the Creator. Revelation 4:11 says, "Thou art worthy, O Lord, to receive glory and honour and power: for thou hast created all things, and for thy pleasure they are and were created." Praise the name of the Lord!

God set boundaries for the seas so that they can come only so far onto the land. The clouds provide a garment for the sea. The depth of the oceans is swaddled in darkness to protect creatures living there. Oceans, seas, rivers, and ponds obey the command of their Creator.

God commands the morning, teaching the dawn its place and spreading the morning westward across the globe to give both day and night.

God has measured the depths of the oceans. He knows every underwater hill and valley. There is not a place on earth He has not been.

God is the only One Who knows what is beyond the gates of death. Very rarely has anyone been permitted a glimpse into the next life. Paul caught a glimpse of the third heaven (II Cor. 12:2-4).

Jesus chose to reveal only bits and pieces to us as in the parable of the rich man and Lazarus the beggar. He told us just enough to calm our fears. There is no need for a child of God to worry about life after death because we know that God is on the other side, too.

This spinning globe we call home is huge, yet we are just one tiny speck in the vast universe. Millions of light-years into space, you would still find the creative power of God at work. What an intriguing thought to wonder where light and darkness reside. But even more intriguing is that God knows the answer.

Snow and hail are part of God's treasury, which He has reserved for times of war. God uses hail as a weapon (Exod. 9:18-26; Josh. 10:11). During the Tribulation, hail and fire will destroy the third part of the trees and grass (Rev. 8:7). During the Battle of Armageddon, God casts hailstones, which weigh one hundred pounds each, to the earth (Rev. 16:21). I believe I will stay on God's side!

God made a way for excess water to run off. What if all the rain stood in puddles without soaking into the ground or running into the streams? We would soon be knee-deep in water. He thought of everything when He created the world.

God also makes a path for the lightning and sends it where it is supposed to go. He is still very much concerned about every least detail and about every creature, including you!

God controls the constellations, which are stable and predictable because of their Creator. God brings forth the seasons with everything planned down to the last detail so that we can sing songs about April showers and May flowers. We get our kites ready for March winds and harvest our crops in the fall. This is an orderly universe because God is a God of design and order.

God, in His loving care, provides food for all the animals. Jesus gently taught His disciples to put their trust in God (Luke 12:22-24). If God provides food for the animals, surely, He will feed us, too.

God knows when all the little animals will be born, and He cares for them. Every baby animal grows up to look like its parents because God commanded every living thing to produce *after its kind*. He did not create monkeys to turn into humans!

Only God could create animals like the peacock and the ostrich. Have you considered lately the diversity of God's creation? Just looking at the different kinds of birds would keep you occupied for a long time.

God points out specific things about the animals as well. The horse did not get its strength from man! God gives flying lessons to the hawk and the eagle. He whispers to the Canadian geese when it is time to migrate. He is the homing device in pigeons and salmon. He is the sonar of bats. God teaches His animals.

Finally, after God lists all these things that He has done, He demands an answer. "Job, you have been contending with Me. You have wanted Me to talk with you. I have given you this quiz, and now it is time for your oral response."

CHAPTER TWENTY-EIGHT
Job Confesses His Ignorance

JOB'S ACCOUNT
JOB 40:3-5

"I am repulsive! Lord, I cannot answer You because I do not know the answers. I will lay my hand on my mouth to keep from speaking any more foolishness. I have already talked too much. I will proceed no further."

Commentary

Good answer! "I am repulsive!" When we stand in the presence of God, we get a good revelation of ourselves. In the light of His majesty and glory, we see ourselves as nothing. In the light of His holiness, we see ourselves as unworthy sinners. When we look into the mirror of His Word, we realize how far short we come to measuring up to the glory of God.

Job has been saying that he wished God would show up; but when God does make Himself known, it scares Job to death. Job realized that he is not as good as he thought. He did not know as many of the answers as he thought. He is not as brave as he boasted he would be about questioning God's motives for his suffering. All he can do in the presence of God is to be quiet and listen, which is the wisest thing possible. In the presence of Someone Who knows all the answers, it is better to just listen.

Even though Job cannot answer the first quiz, God gives him a second one. Again, God appears in the whirlwind, hurling questions right and left. God still does not answer any of Job's questions; but in light of the weighty questions of God, Job's questions seem petty, anyway.

But God is not finished with Job just yet. He still has more to reveal to him.

CHAPTER TWENTY-NINE
God Reveals His Power

GOD'S ACCOUNT
JOB 40:6–41:34

"Job, act like a man, and I will ask another round of questions for you to answer. Are you stronger than I? Are you able to annul my judgment? Can you, by condemning Me, make yourself righteous? Is your arm as strong as Mine, or is your voice able to roar like the thunder of My voice?

"Can you prove your superior strength? Adorn yourself with majesty and excellency and clothe yourself with glory and beauty. Fling your anger over the face of the earth to bring down those prideful men. Crush all the wicked, bury them in the dust, and hide their evil deeds. When you are able to do all these things, I will confess that you, by your own right hand, can save yourself.

"Why did I create such an ugly and useless animal as the hippopotamus? Look at him. I made him along with you so that you both are the work of My hand. He eats grass like an ox, yet he is not an ox. His strength is in his thighs and stomach, yet that power cannot be harnessed for labor. He moves his tail, and it looks like a cedar tree swinging. His muscles are powerful, and his bones are as strong as brass and bars of iron.

"Job, the hippopotamus is My favorite animal because he displays My grace to other ugly and useless creatures. He and I play sword games together! The mountains provide his food; he lays around in the shade of the trees; and he wallows up to his nose in the reeds of the brook. He slowly drinks up a river fully convinced that he can swallow the Jordan! He sees everything. His nose pierces through snares.

"What about the sea creatures? Can you control one of them? Can you catch him with a fish hook, put a hook in his nose, or bore a hole through his jaw with a thorn? Does he bring his prayer requests to you, or does he whisper softly in your ear? Will he make a covenant with you to be your servant? Can you, or perhaps your maids, keep his as a family pet? Do your friends serve fried crocodile at their banquets?

"Is it possible for you to kill him with barbed irons or fishing spears? Lay your hand on him one time, and you will remember that experience for the rest of your life. If you survive, you will never do it again! Your hope of catching him is foolish; he scares you to death just looking at him. No one is brave enough to stir him up. If you are afraid of one of My little creatures, how will you be able to stand before Me, the Creator of all things?

"To whom do I owe anything? Is there anyone to whom I am under obligation to repay a debt? I own everything under the whole heaven! It all belongs to Me!

"Look at the crocodile. Who can understand the features and the power of the crocodile? I am going to show you his parts, power, and purpose. Who can so much as discover what his skin looks like, yet even catch him? Who can open his mouth? His teeth are ferocious! He is proud of his scales because they are so tightly sealed together that no air can come between them. They stick together like a plate of armor that cannot be pierced.

"When he sneezes, light shines out of his eyes like the rays of the morning. Fire goes out of his mouth like a burning flame, and smoke comes out of his nostrils like a boiling cauldron so that his breath kindles a fire. His neck is strong so that he gets his way in everything. The folds of his skin are firm and immovable, and his heart is as hard as stone without caring or compassion.

Mighty men are afraid of him; when they see him coming, they repent! Swords, spears, darts, and javelins have no effect on him.

"When he travels on land, his belly is like sharp stones making tracks in the mud; when he swims, he churns up the sea like a boiling pot. In his wake, the sea looks white-headed! Upon all the earth, there is none to compare with him in his fearlessness and pride. He oversees all the high things of the earth."

Commentary

God reveals so much of Himself through these series of questions. For one thing, God has a strong arm! "The LORD hath made bare his holy arm in the eyes of all the nations; and all the ends of the earth shall see the salvation of our God" (Isa. 52:10). God has rolled up His sleeves to fight for His people, and all the nations of the earth will be aware of His mighty power!

If you are on the Lord's side, He uses that strong arm in your behalf. "For the eyes of the LORD run to and fro throughout the whole earth, to shew himself strong in the behalf of them whose heart is perfect toward him" (II Chron. 16:9). Isaiah 59:1 declares, "Behold, the LORD's hand is not shortened, that it cannot save; neither his ear heavy, that it cannot hear." God has lost none of His power. He is still a strong God!

Man is just as weak as God is strong. Would all the ladies not like to be able to clothe themselves with beauty (yes—and most of the men, too). But we are the way God made us. We might put on some paint or wear some expensive clothes, but there is very little about our outward appearance that we can change. "And which of you with taking thought can add to his stature one cubit? If ye then be not able to do that thing which is least, why take ye thought for the rest?" (Luke 12:25-26). Matthew 5:36 says, "Neither shalt thou swear by thy head, because thou canst not make one hair white or black." You might dye your hair, but the roots will still be the color God made them!

God asks Job, "Are you strong enough to crush the wicked?" Job had asked God why the wicked prosper; and in effect, God is telling him that it is none of his business. In *The Chronicles of Narnia*, C.S. Lewis has one of the characters explain to the children that Aslan the Lion never tells you anyone else's story. He only tells you your own. God seems to be telling Job that if he wants the wicked crushed, then Job should do it. God is the Judge and not man. Who would be left if man had the power to crush all he considered wicked?

God tells Job that when he is able to crush all the wicked, then he will be powerful enough to save himself. But God knows that both are impossible. We cannot change others, and we cannot save ourselves. That is why we need God.

Then, God turns things into something quite humorous. He compares man to a hippopotamus! That should take some of the pride out of us. Both man and the hippopotamus are ugly and useless, but both are created by the same God.

God says that the hippo is His favorite animal—presumably because he is a display of God's grace. If God loves something so ugly and so useless, perhaps He can love me, too. If God treats the hippo as a favorite pet, surely there is enough grace to reach me. Not only does God love the hippo, but He also plays games with him. Can you get a mental picture of God playing sword games with a hippopotamus? I wonder which one plays the good guy.

Sometimes, we are too serious with God. He can be fun, laidback, and carefree. The next time you begin to take yourself too seriously, stop and think about a God Who plays sword games with hippos! God enjoys the work of His hands. He looked at His finished creation and saw "it was very good" (Gen. 1:31). May God be able to look upon you and me and find pleasure in us.

Not only does God enjoy His creation, but He also knows them in intimate detail. There is nothing about you that God does not know—your fears, your insecurities, your weaknesses, your temptations, your strong points, and your abilities. You do not have to hide things when you enter His presence.

He already knows and loves you regardless. Come before God honestly, and He will help you work through all the things that are wrong in your life. God wants to be involved in our lives. Psalm 103:13-14 tells us, "Like as a father pitieth his children, so the LORD pitieth them that fear him. For he knoweth our frame; he remembereth that we are dust." Just like a loving Father, He wants to help us mature.

Does a sea creature pray? Do we? Are you afraid of sea monsters? Are you equally afraid of God? God owns everything. "For every beast of the forest in mine, and the cattle upon a thousand hills. I know all the fowls of the mountains: and the wild beasts of the field are mine. If I were hungry, I would not tell thee: for the world is mine, and the fulness thereof" (Psalm 50:10-12). Psalm 24:1 proclaims, "The earth is the LORD's, and the fulness thereof; the world, and they that dwell therein." "Behold, all souls are mine; as the soul of the father, so also the soul of the son is mine: the soul that sinneth, it shall die" (Ezek. 18:4).

Now, as if to prove to Job that He really does own everything, God goes into great detail describing the crocodile. One of the great descriptions refers to him having his sorrow turned into joy, perhaps saying that he gets his way in everything. When you are that big, you can pretty well get whatever you want! It is comforting to realize that God knows all of His creatures. But toward the end of this description, God seems to change gears: "He beholdeth all high things: he is a king over all the children of pride" (Job 41:34).

Pride is a characteristic the crocodile shares with Satan, who is the prince of pride.

> How art thou fallen from heaven, O Lucifer, son of the morning! how art thou cut down to the ground, which didst weaken the nations! For thou hast said in thine heart, I will ascend into heaven, I will exalt my throne above the stars of God: I will sit also upon the mount of the congregation, in the sides of the north: I will ascend above the heights of the clouds; I will be

like the most High. Yet thou shalt be brought down to hell, to the sides of the pit (Isa. 14:12-15).

Ezekiel 28:15-17 also says, "Thou wast perfect in thy ways from the day that thou wast created, till iniquity was found in thee . . . Thine heart was lifted up because of thy beauty, thou hast corrupted thy wisdom by reason of the brightness." Satan was cast out of Heaven because of his pride.

Now, we may wonder why God allows such monsters (the crocodile and Satan) to exist and threaten man. Why does God not destroy all evil? It seems that evil is necessary in order to test men. If there were no evil, there would be no option but to do right. God wants men to love Him because they choose to—not because they are forced to from lack of a choice.

God did not create us to be robots He could control by the push of a button. He gave us the awesome gift of freedom of choice. All men must decide whether or not they will love and serve God. God, in His own time, will put down all evil and usher in a kingdom of righteousness which will last for eternity. Until then, let us remember that all things are under God's power and control (including Satan and the crocodile). Let us put our faith and trust in the Sovereign God and rest in His ability. Faith in God brings peace to the ash heap!

CHAPTER THIRTY
Job Worships

JOB'S ACCOUNT
JOB 42:1-6

"Lord, I have learned that You can do everything! You have revealed Your mighty power and given us examples through Your creation, so I am convinced there is nothing impossible with You. I have also learned that You know everything. You know when I am suffering, and You have not forsaken me like I thought. You knew the anguish of my friend's criticism and lies. You know my secret heart. You know my every thought. Oh, great God, You know everything!

"I have also learned some things about myself. I wanted to know all the answers so badly that I did not wait for You to reveal Yourself. In my impatience, I have been very foolish. I have spoken words without knowing their meaning. I grasped for answers that were way over my head. I asked questions about things I had no business being curious about.

"Lord, let me start all over. If You could just erase all my past blunders and let me start fresh, I would try to do better. Hear me please; I beg You. I have heard about You with my ears; but now that I have seen You for myself, I hate myself for being such a fool. Lord, I am sorry. Please forgive me. I repent in dust and ashes. I humble myself before You and plead for Your mercy."

Commentary

Such a holy moment when a person catches sight of the true and living God. What a learning experience just to sit still at the feet of our Lord and listen to His Word. When Jesus was visiting in the home of Mary, Martha, and Lazarus, Martha got frustrated with the preparation of a meal for her honored guest. She looked around for some assistance from her sister Mary and saw her sitting at the feet of Jesus, listening to his teaching.

> But Martha was cumbered about much serving, and came to him, and said, Lord, dost thou not care that my sister hath left me to serve alone? bid her therefore that she help me. And Jesus answered and said unto her, Martha, Martha, thou art careful and troubled about many things: But one thing is needful: and Mary hath chosen that good part, which shall not be taken away from her" (Luke 10:40-42).

Jesus said that there was only one thing which is absolutely essential—hearing the Word. May the Holy Spirit impress upon our hearts the need for communion with God through prayer, Bible study, and church attendance. Only as we spend time with the great Teacher will we learn the really important lessons about God, about ourselves, and about others. While God was speaking, Job was listening carefully; and he proves what a good student he is by the answers he gives about what he has learned.

Job learns that God is omnipotent. He is all-powerful. While God spoke about His creation, Job's faith grew until he came to believe God can do anything.

For almost twenty years, Abraham and Sarah had lived with the promise that God would give them a son, but now it was too late. Abraham was old, and Sarah was no longer able to bear children. Sarah had given up hope of ever holding that little boy in her arms and singing him to sleep. But the Lord spoke to Abraham:

> And he said, I will certainly return unto thee according to the time of life; and, lo, Sarah thy wife shall have a son. And Sarah heard it in the tent door, which was behind him . . . Therefore Sarah laughed within herself, saying, After I am waxed old shall I have pleasure, my lord being old also? And the LORD said unto Abraham, Wherefore did Sarah laugh, saying, Shall I of a surety bear a child, which am old? Is any thing too hard for the LORD? At the time appointed I will return unto thee, according to the time of life, and Sarah shall have a son (Gen. 18:10-14).

Just to prove that nothing is too hard for God and that God always keeps His promises, "the LORD visited Sarah as he had said, and the LORD did unto Sarah as he had spoken. For Sarah conceived, and bare Abraham a son in his old age, at the set time of which God had spoken to him" (Gen. 21:1-2).

God did what He said He would do. There is nothing too hard for God! Those two elderly people sat in their nursery holding their son with tears running down their faces. But they are tears of joy and laughter, so much so that they named that little boy Isaac, which means "laughter." God had turned their laughter of doubt and unbelief into the laughter of joy.

The angel Gabriel came to announce that Mary had been chosen to be the one who would give birth to the Messiah. As if to prove the validity of his message, Gabriel revealed the news that Mary's cousin Elizabeth had conceived a child in her old age after a lifetime of barrenness. The angel explained, "For with God nothing shall be impossible" (Luke 1:37).

Jesus had been teaching about how hard it was for a rich man to enter the Kingdom of Heaven, and the disciples "were astonished, saying . . . Who then can be saved? And Jesus looking upon them saith, With men it is impossible, but not with God: for with God all things are possible" (Mark 10:26-27). There is nothing too hard for God!

God is also omniscient. He knows everything. "Remember the former things of old: for I am God, and there is none else; I am God, and there is none like me, Declaring the end from the beginning, and from ancient times the things that are not yet done, saying, My counsel shall stand, and I will do all my pleasure" (Isa. 46:9-10). God knows the end from the beginning! He inspired His prophets to record things which would happen one thousand years in the future. Indeed, God has given us a record in His Word of things which are yet in the future. Because He knows the future, I need not worry about tomorrow.

God knows everything about you and me. If He keeps a record of the number of hairs on our head and knows every time one comes out in the shower, surely, He knows other areas of our lives equally well. He knows our hurts and disappointments, our joys and successes. He knows all about us!

When Job saw a revelation of God, his questions became unimportant. The focus of his life was no longer "Why?" but "Who?" We make the statement, "When I get home, I'm going to ask God about that." But instead, we will be just like Job. When we see *Him*, all our questions will seem trivial. We will just bow on our knees with the angels around the throne saying, "Holy, holy, holy, LORD God Almighty, which was, and is, and is to come . . . Worthy is the Lamb that was slain to receive power, and riches, and wisdom, and strength, and honour, and glory, and blessing . . . Blessing, and honour, and glory, and power, be unto him that sitteth upon the throne, and unto the Lamb for ever and ever" (Rev. 4:8, 5:12-13). Just to see the Lord our God will be enough. In His presence, the questions are not important.

In the presence of God, Job learns some things about himself also. He was impatient, wanting God to reveal Himself so badly that he said some foolish things and made some dumb accusations against God. When we stand in the presence of God, we get a good picture of ourselves. In comparison with God, we are so puny and insignificant that we wonder why God even bothers with us. The person who can stand and boast on himself during his prayers has never seen God. The person who is compelled to spend his life listing his own accomplishments and boasting of his own achievements has never stood before a holy God and seen the works of His hands. For in the presence of God, our illusions of self-importance crumble. John the Baptist said it best: "He must increase, but I must decrease" (John 3:30). John had truly seen the Christ!

Job had previously had secondhand knowledge of God. "I have heard of thee by the hearing of the ear" (Job 42:5). So many people only know what someone else has told them about Jesus. Grandmother sat in her rocking chair and sang the songs of redemption. Mom and Dad told the grand, old stories of the heroes of faith. Pastor preached about the love of God and the redemptive work of Christ Jesus on the cross. But up to that point, everything we know about God is secondhand.

We have the Word in our head. We have memorized verses of Scripture, but we need a personal experience with the King of kings. Job said, "But now mine eye seeth thee" (Job 42:5). What a difference it makes going from head knowledge to heart knowledge! A person can know everything there is to know about God and still die and go to Hell. But someone can know nothing except the blood of Jesus and be saved! It is that personal relationship with God that counts.

When you know God personally, you have "a peace . . . which passeth all understanding" (Phil. 4:7). You do not have to depend on someone else's description; you know for yourself. You realize that despite all the testimony you have heard about Jesus, the half has never been told. You do not have to rely on someone's opinion about God. Christ has come into your life, and you have the assurance that nothing can take that away.

Then, Job prayed a powerful prayer of repentance. He humbled himself in the dust, asking for God's forgiveness. The story of the Pharisee, who boasted on himself in his prayers, talks about another man who knew his own condition. The Pharisee thought he knew himself; the publican really did. "And the publican, standing afar off, would not lift up so much as his eyes unto heaven, but smote upon his breast, saying, God be merciful to me a sinner. I tell you, this man went down to his house justified rather than the other: for every one that exalteth himself shall be abased; and he that humbleth himself shall be exalted" (Luke 18:13-14).

The publican went home justified! God recognized his right to be included in the family of God. We can be justified freely by the shed blood of Jesus and are able to come into the presence of God as one of His children!

Job is still sitting on the ash heap, still covered with boils, and still scraping himself with a broken piece of pottery. Nothing on the outside has changed, but everything is different. Faith has prevailed! Hope in God has brought Job through the test. Job was willing to hang in there until God came; and when God showed up, nothing else mattered. Only, give me Jesus! There is still evil in the world, but I believe in God. I am still suffering, but I believe in God. I still do not understand why, but I believe in God!

Now that God has dealt with Job, He turns his attention to the three friends.

CHAPTER THIRTY-ONE
God Rebukes Job's Friends

GOD'S ACCOUNT
JOB 42:7-9

"Eliphaz the Temanite, I am very angry with you and your two friends because you have not spoken the truth about Me like My servant Job has. Therefore, I command you to take seven bulls and seven rams and go to My servant Job. In his presence, offer up a sacrifice of burnt offering for yourselves. Then have My servant Job pray for you, and I will accept his prayers on your behalf. If you refuse to follow these guidelines, I will deal with you according to your foolishness; for you have not spoken the truth about Me like My servant Job has."

Commentary

God is teaching Job's three friends some powerful lessons here that we all need to learn.

Lesson #1: If you want to make God angry, pervert the truth.

Eliphaz and his three friends have not been interested in truth; they only wanted to win the debate and sway Job to their way of thinking. Often in the heat of the argument, we forget about the truth and focus only on winning. Churches have fought for years over petty differences in doctrine. Is the rapture of the Church pre-millennial, post-millennial, or amillennial? Even among those who believe in a pre-millennial rapture, there are opposing camps: pre-tribulationists, post-tribulationists, and mid-tribulationists. I happen to be a pre-millennial pre-tribulationist, and I will spend the next fifty years proving that I am right! But seriously, would it not be much better for the body of Christ to unite around the fundamental truths of the Word of God and spend our time telling sinners about the saving power of the blood of Jesus instead of fighting over minor points of contention? Jesus is coming when the Father tells Him to come, and our duty is just to be ready to go when He calls.

The Father gets very angry when men pervert the truth. Eliphaz and his three friends misrepresented God by accusing Job of sin. They were convinced that suffering was a symptom of sin, and they were willing to debate until they were blue in the face to prove their argument.

Many pastors march into their pulpits on Sunday mornings armed with facts, figures, and surveys to prove that God is not Who the Bible says He is. We have watered down the truth to make it acceptable to a wider range of people. We have softened the punch of the Bible to gain members, dollars, or prestige in the community. We have taken the blood of Jesus out of our songs and sermons and pushed the Holy Spirit out of our services in favor of a form and a fashion. We have tried to modernize the Gospel but have succeeded only in turning our churches into social clubs with no power to minister to the needs of people and change their lives with the truth.

Truth will still set you free (John 8:32)! May the Holy Spirit anoint His ministers again with the resolution to preach the Word of God, even if they have to stand on a tree stump to do it. May God also give us men with enough backbone to preach the uncompromising truth!

Those who have watered down and perverted the truth will one day come face to face with an angry God. All the numbers, the money, and the prestige of men will vanish like leaves before the wind as a Holy God speaks judgment against them. "Then shall he say also unto them on the left hand, Depart from me, ye cursed, into everlasting fire, prepared for the devil and his angels" (Matt. 25:41). Matthew 7:15-23 warns:

> Beware of false prophets, which come to you in sheep's clothing, but inwardly they are ravening wolves . . . Not everyone that saith unto me, Lord, Lord, shall enter into the kingdom of heaven; but he that doeth the will of my Father which is in heaven. Many will say to me in that day, Lord, Lord, have we not prophesied in thy name? and in thy name have cast out devils? and in thy name done many wonderful works? And then will I profess unto them, I never knew you: depart from me, ye that work iniquity.

There is a very solemn warning here: if you are going to speak for God, learn the truth first and be committed to teaching the truth, regardless of the cost. Only the truth will set men free.

Lesson #2: If you want to appease the wrath of God, repent.

God gave Job's friends three specifics for repentance. First, they had to apologize. It is time to "eat crow." Churches once taught new converts the act of restitution—making amends for past sins as much as possible. The converted thief was encouraged to repay what he had stolen. The gossip and the liar were supposed to set the record straight. The new convert was taught to correct as many of his past mistakes as he possibly could in order for his testimony as a Christian to not be hindered by past grudges or hurts.

God still demands restitution for those who want to make progress in their Christian walk. God has vindicated Job; and now, He demands an apology from Eliphaz, Bildad, and Zophar. Repentance also involves some tangible expression of being sorry for the sins that have been committed. In this case, the three friends of Job were to offer seven bulls and seven rams as a burnt offering.

In Exodus 29:15-18, we find directions for this kind of offering. The person making the offering was to put his hands on the animal's head, symbolically identifying with the suffering of the animal and the transferring of his sins to the sacrifice. Thus, when the priest slit the throat of the animal, it was if he had slit the throat and spilled the blood of the sinner.

Death has always been the penalty for sin. "For the wages of sin is death" (Rom. 6:23). But in this case, God said that He would accept the death of an animal as a substitute for the death of the man who had sinned. Next, the priest was to sprinkle the blood of the sacrificial animal on the brazen altar. God recognized blood as a covering for sin (the Old Testament word "atonement") so that when He saw the sprinkled blood of the sacrificial animal, He accepted it on behalf of the sinner. The animal was butchered, washed (another symbol of cleansing), and burned on the brazen altar. The entire animal was to be consumed by the flames of the altar, showing that the offense was completely absolved.

So, when God commanded Job's three friends to offer a burnt offering, it was a call to repentance. God still demands repentance for those who would come to Him. It is not enough to shake a preacher's hand or sign a card of decision. There must be a turning away from sin and a turning toward God. There was a time when Holy Ghost convictions gripped the hearts of sinners, and they would walk down a church aisle to an old-fashioned altar with tears streaming down their faces. They would pray a sinner's prayer with conviction. When they stood with the glow of God's forgiveness on their face, you knew they had experienced God. You knew that God had forgiven their sins, and they were a different person. There must be genuine repentance when a guilty person stands before a holy God.

But repentance is not just for sinners. Jesus taught us to pray daily, "Forgive us our debts" (Matt. 6:12). As we walk on this earth, we need to keep short accounts with God by seeking His forgiveness often. "If my people, which are called by my name, shall humble themselves, and pray, and seek my face, and turn from their wicked ways; then will I hear from heaven, and will forgive their sin, and will heal their land" (II Chron. 7:14). If all those who call themselves Christian would put away their sin, pride, selfishness, and petty differences and seek the face of God together as His children, there would be a mighty revival in our land.

Christians can be intercessors for the sins of their nation. Read the great prayer of Ezra in Ezra 9:5-15 as he confesses the sins of the nation of Israel and prays for mercy. We, too, need to pray for our country and seek the face of God for our leaders so that we as a nation may yet return to God before it is too late. "I exhort therefore, that, first of all, supplications, prayers, intercessions, and giving of thanks, be made for all men; For kings, and for all that are in authority; that we may lead a quiet and peaceable life in all godliness and honesty" (I Tim. 2:1-2).

The third thing God demanded was that Eliphaz, Bildad, and Zophar ask Job to pray for them. Through this whole debate, they have been mocking Job as a sinner; and now, God tells them that Job is more righteous than they are. What a humbling experience when we see ourselves through God's eyes, yet we will never know ourselves any other way. May God shine the searchlight of His love on our lives and allow us to see ourselves as we really are. May He give us grace to repent so that we can mature in Christ.

To their eternal credit, Eliphaz, Bildad, and Zophar did exactly as God instructed them. True to the faith that has brought him thus far in this epic story, Job graciously accepted his friends' apology, forgave them, and prayed for them. "And the LORD turned the captivity of Job, when he prayed for his friends" (Job 42:10).

Lesson #3: You can turn your captivity around.

One of the things which brought about a reversal of Job's situation was forgiveness. Job is still sitting on the ash heap scraping his boils. He has become somewhat bitter against God because of his physical suffering and frustrated with his friends because of their criticism and mockery. But Job finds peace and healing for his wounded spirit through forgiveness. God accepted Job when Job accepted the apology of his friends.

A person will never survive as a Christian unless he learns to forgive. There is enough anger, bitterness, and backstabbing in the world to kill us all if we let it. But there is also enough grace to forgive. Forgiveness is opening the prison doors to set the prisoner free and discovering that the prisoner was you. "For if ye forgive men their trespasses, your heavenly Father will also forgive you: But if ye forgive not men their trespasses, neither will your Father forgive your trespasses" (Matt. 6:14-15).

The second thing which brought about a reversal of Job's situation was praying for his enemies. "Confess your faults one to another, and pray one for another, that ye may be healed. The effectual fervent prayer of a righteous man availeth much" (James 5:16). When we can get beyond our selfishness long enough to pray for others, God sends healing to our own souls. Many people are so preoccupied with self that there is no room for anything else in their lives, including healing and deliverance from God. But Job looked away from his suffering long enough to minister to the needs of his friends; and while Job was not looking, God slipped in to minister to Job's needs.

EPILOGUE
God Restores Job

JOB 42:10-17

"And the Lord turned the captivity of Job, when he prayed for his friends: also the LORD gave Job twice as much as he had before" (Job 42:10). What a beautiful picture of the grace of God with a powerful example of what faith in God can do. Job has passed the test!

His faith has prevailed though the time of trial. He held on to God when all the odds were against him. He lost all his material possessions; his children died; his wife wished him dead; his friends accused him of sin; and it seemed that God was a million miles away. But through it all, Job clung tenaciously to his faith. Now, God chooses to doubly bless him!

Remember that this is Job's story—not yours. This is not a promise that your situation will turn out as rosy as Job's. God may choose to take you home before He turns your situation around, *but keep holding on.* Faith will prevail! Even if nothing changes in this life, keep your hand tightly in the hand of the Master. Keep your faith anchored to the Rock of Ages. Keep your eyes on Jesus. Keep on running this race with patience. When the Lord Jesus Christ, the Captain of our salvation, leads you through those pearly gates into the presence of God the Father, He will turn your captivity, too.

God chose to give Job a reversal in this life. He lifted the agonizing weight of grief. When Job prayed for his friends, God set Job's soul free from the bondage of bitterness and frustration. Like a bird loosed from its cage, Job's spirit soared into the heavens above the chaos, strife, pain, and suffering. Job must have stood up and shouted that day because it is hard to sit still and be quiet when God lifts that kind of load off your soul. Blessed be the name of the Lord!

God healed his body. Those ghastly sores dried up; Job's skin became clear; and the horrible itching stopped. Job dropped the broken piece of pottery and lifted his hands in praise to God for restored health.

God restored his relationship with his wife. She, who had been so distraught she would not let Job comfort her, reached out in shared love so that they were able to have more children.

"Also the LORD gave Job twice as much as he had before . . . So the LORD blessed the latter end of Job more than his beginning: for he had fourteen thousand sheep, and six thousand camels, and a thousand yoke of oxen, and a thousand she asses. He had also seven sons and three daughters" (Job 42:10, 12-13).

God restored the losses that Job had suffered by giving him double what he had at the beginning of the test. God doubled his sheep, camels, oxen, and asses. In fact, God gave Job double of everything, except his children. Death can take the physical presence of our loved ones away from us, but it can never take *them*—those precious memories we cherish and the love that still exists in our hearts for them. God did not double the number of Job's children because there was nothing that could take the place of the ones he lost. Besides, they are not lost when you know where they are!

"Then came there unto him all his brethren, and all his sisters, and all they that had been of his acquaintance before, and did eat bread with him in his house: and they bemoaned him, and comforted him over all the evil that the LORD had brought upon him: every man also gave him a piece of money, and every one an earring of gold" (Job 42:11). God blessed Job with a reunion with his former family and friends, but notice that they did not come around until after God had restored Job's wealth.

Job was very gracious in dealing with these fair-weather friends, but where were Job's brothers when he needed someone to defend him against the accusations of his friends? Where were Job's sisters when he needed a shoulder to cry on? Where were all these acquaintances when Job needed medical attention? They only show up in order to feed on Job's bread again. They only show up after the fact to moan and groan and offer "comfort." They were not around to identify with the suffering while it was in progress, but they want to glory in the horrid details now that all the danger is past. They ran from the suffering; but now, they want to share in the glory of restoration.

In all fairness to these guests, they did contribute a piece of money and an earring of gold to Job's account. But you wonder if this is not just a bribe to get back in his good graces now that Job is a rich man again. Certainly, he does not need their money now that he is twice as wealthy as before. Where were they with their offerings a few days ago when Job had lost everything and could have used their support? This group gathered around Job's supper table looks a lot like parasites.

God extended Job's life. "After this lived Job an hundred and forty years, and saw his sons, and his sons' sons, even four generations" (Job 42:16). God gave Job a second chance at life. He lived another 140 years. (Was Job 140 years old when this testing began? Since God doubled everything else, did He double Job's lifespan, too?) At any rate, God gave him many wonderful years after the time of testing was over.

Job looked around many times on his blessings and thanked God for not taking his life when he prayed to die. Look what Job would have missed if God had answered that prayer. Perhaps you, too, think there is no reason to live any longer. You wish God would come and take you away. Or perhaps you have thought about ending your own life. Please hold on to life. Please do not give in now. You never know what is just around the corner. You might be surprised with what tomorrow holds.

Job named his three daughters Jemima, Kezia, and Kerenhappuch. Even their names reflect the change from grief to joy. Jemima means "Lovely as the Day." Kezia is a fragrance. Kerenhappuch means "the Horn of Color." These girls brought beauty, fragrance, and color back to Job's life. They were beautiful girls, and Job gave them an inheritance along with their brothers. Usually, the inheritance was divided among the sons, but Job loved all his children and treated them equally.

Job lived to see his grandchildren and his great-grandchildren. He probably had bumper stickers on his ox carts that said, "Ask me about my grandchildren" and "Let me tell you about my great-grandchildren." What a blessing for him to see the progression of the generations and to be around to influence them for good! How we need godly grandparents to teach those little ones about Jesus.

Paul, the apostle, said to young Timothy, who had been called to pastor the church at Ephesus, "When I call to remembrance the unfeigned faith that is in thee, which dwelt first in thy grandmother Lois, and thy mother Eunice; and I am persuaded that in thee also" (II Tim. 1:5). Through a grandmother and a mother, faith had been passed on to the one who would pastor the new congregation of Ephesus and bring many souls into the kingdom of God. How wonderful it is to be able to pass our faith on to the next generation.

"So Job died, being old and full of days" (Job 42:17). A man who had faced life with an unshakable faith in God now stood in the presence of God and for the first time understood the "why." Job never knew the whole story until he got home. He was not allowed to see the contest between God and Satan during the testing.

Perhaps all the way to the end, Job continued to believe that God had sent the pain and suffering. But now, he knows. Now, he understands clearly the pain and the suffering. He rejoices in the fact that his faith, which has been tried through the fire, is now pure gold. He presents that pure gold as an offering to God in praise and worship for bringing him home safely.

When Job died, the angels of God came to carry his spirit into the bosom of Abraham (Luke 16:22). There in Paradise, Job's spirit rested in peace and comfort until the day of Jesus' resurrection when Job was transported from Paradise into Heaven with all the rest of the Old Testament saints.

First Peter 3:18-19 says, "For Christ also hath once suffered for sins, the just for the unjust, that he might bring us to God, being put to death in the flesh, but quickened by the Spirit: By which also he went and preached unto the spirits in prison." At the resurrection of Jesus from the dead, He transported all those in the bosom of Abraham into the bosom of the Father.

Today, Job is still in Heaven in the presence of God, waiting for that day of resurrection when his spirit will be reunited with his glorified body. At the rapture of the Church, Jesus our Lord will bring Job's spirit back with Him. When the trumpet sounds, all the graves of those who died in Christ will burst open, and their bodies will be resurrected. Christ will reunite Job's glorified body with his spirit, and Job will live forever in the presence of God in his glorified body (I Thess. 4:13-18).

Job said that *in his flesh*, he would see God. On that day of resurrection, he will become a body of flesh and bone like the resurrected body of Jesus.

> And as they thus spake, Jesus himself stood in the midst of them, and saith unto them, Peace be unto you. But they were terrified and affrighted, and supposed that they had seen a spirit. And he said unto them, Why are ye troubled? and why do thoughts arise in your hearts? Behold my hands and my feet, that it is I myself: handle me, and see; for a spirit hath not flesh and bones, as ye see me have (Luke 24:36-39).

Job is still waiting for fulfillment of the promise of a Redeemer Who will stand on this earth in the latter days. Jesus is coming again to set up a kingdom of peace and righteousness on the earth. But that is sometime in the future. For now, Job is content that the pain and suffering are over. The heartache and the tears of this life are left far behind, and Job is at rest in a place of peace and happiness.

A Word of Encouragement

We have learned from the Book of Job that life is not always easy and that our friends sometimes do not understand. The person who said that when you come to Jesus, all of your problems would be over was wrong. Sometimes, just being a Christian creates problems! The doctrine which teaches that a child of God never has to suffer does not hold true in the real world. God never promised a life of ease and comfort. In fact, the opposite is almost true. "But if, when ye do well, and suffer for it, ye take it patiently, this is acceptable with God. For even hereunto were ye called: because Christ also suffered for us, leaving us an example, that ye should follow his steps" (I Peter 2:20-21). "Yea, and all that will live godly in Christ Jesus shall suffer persecution" (II Tim. 3:12).

Sometimes, the road is rough and rocky. Sometimes, the mountain seems too steep to climb. Sometimes, the things we go through are unpleasant. But we have a promise from our precious Savior: "Lo, I am with you always, even unto the end of the world. Amen" (Matt. 28:20). We have His assurance that we will never walk this road alone. Whatever we are going through, the One Who created this world will go through it with us. "Yea, though I walk through the valley of the shadow of death, I will fear no evil: for thou art with me" (Psalm 23:4).

There is one more promise we need to remember. "There hath no temptation taken you but such as is common to man: but God is faithful, who will not suffer you to be tempted above that ye are able; but will with the temptation also make a way to escape, that ye may be able to bear it" (I Cor. 10:13). God will never put more on us than we are able to bear. Satan will never be allowed to push us past the breaking point: he can only afflict us by special permission from the Father. Whatever God has given Satan permission to do in our lives will become a test of our character and a trial of our faith.

Several years ago, the company I was working for declared bankruptcy; and the trial judge ordered the plant closed and the doors locked. The message came to us about 3:30 in the afternoon, and we were given thirty minutes to get our personal things together and leave the building. Since I had parked a good distance away from the plant, I went to my car, planning to drive up to the closest access to my office so that I could load my personal things and leave. I got in the car and turned on the ignition, and I heard over my car radio the words to "Amazing Grace."

That has been many years ago, but I still feel the presence of the Lord when I remember that He was there with a word of comfort when I needed Him. I had two small children and a stay-at-home wife, and I was responsible for putting food on the table and clothes on their backs. But God had the record cued to the third verse of "Amazing Grace" to let me know that I was not alone and that everything would work out all right if I would just keep my faith in Him.

Oh, what strength that gave me in the days ahead when I was looking for work. I knew that I was not alone. God was looking for work with me! God had sent a word of encouragement that I could hold close to my heart and a promise that I could lean on during the hard places. That sign from God was enough to cause faith to rise up in my spirit and to keep me from feeling depressed and fearful.

Just recently, I went through a very similar experience. The company I was working for laid off fifty of its managers, including me. Quite suddenly, I was again without a job. When I got to my car, there was no song of hope.

There was no voice of comfort. There was no sign from God that everything would be all right. But I had already been through it once and had learned that God is trustworthy. There was not a voice, just a deep abiding peace in my heart that God is in control.

I know now that everything which comes our way has been approved by our Father. I was convinced that Romans 8:28 is still true: "And we know that all things work together for good to them that love God, to them who are the called according to his purpose."

When I got home with the news, my wife had her own story to tell. That very morning during her time of devotions, God had spoken to her heart with a promise that He was going to open the windows of Heaven for us and bless us.

I am still unemployed, but I believe God. My faith in Him is strong, and I know that He will work out every situation for His honor and glory. Perhaps the rapture of the Church is about to take place, and I will not need a job. Maybe God will provide the means for me to pastor full-time, or maybe He will direct me to another job. At this point, I do not know God's plan; I just know God, and that is enough.

Are you going through a time of suffering? Are you feeling the strain of pain and heartache? I would encourage you to hold on to God with all your might. Let your faith reach out to the Christ of Calvary, Who gave His life to save your soul. Put your hope and trust in the nail-pierced hand of the Savior. Home is just around the bend. One day soon, this rocky road you are traveling on will turn to gold; and you will be rejoicing around the throne of God.

Your journey of faith is almost over. One day, you will stand before almighty God and hear Him say, "Well done, thou good and faithful servant: thou hast been faithful over a few things, I will make thee ruler over many things: enter thou into the joy of thy lord" (Matt. 25:21). You will then be able to say, "It has been worth it all. My faith has been tested and tried. I have gone through the fire. But I am home now, and every step of the way has been worth taking."

Go with God. Fight the good fight of faith. Keep your eyes on Jesus. I will meet you around the throne of God when our journey of faith is finished.

Acknowledgments

I am very grateful to all the people who attend Central Full Gospel Church and for the privilege of being your pastor for the past forty-one years. The responsibility of preaching and teaching three times each week has forced me to diligently study the Word of God. You have been a blessing by your faithful attendance and by your love and support for me and my family. I love you all!

I am thankful for my three amazing daughters, my three wonderful sons-in-law, and my seven grandchildren who continue to amaze me with their talent, intelligence, and love for their papa/grandpa.

About the Author

Bobby Norman was saved when he was eleven years old. He felt the call to preach at an early age and preached his first "sermon" when he was thirteen. He played the piano for a gospel group for several years, then began pastoring at the age of twenty-three and served as a bi-vocational pastor for over forty years.

In 2015, he retired as the knitting manager for a textile plant but continued as a full-time pastor at Central Full Gospel Church in State Road, North Carolina. Bobby is also the vice president of his local ministerial association and volunteers for Lifeline Pregnancy Help Center, where he teaches "Dads Matter" classes for expectant fathers. He has also published two other books: *In the Days When Judges Ruled* and *The Generations of Adam*.

He and his wife, Barbara, have been married for fifty-two years. They are blessed with three grown daughters and seven grandchildren.

For more information about
BOBBY NORMAN
please visit:

www.bobbywnormanauthor.com

Ambassador International's mission is to magnify the Lord Jesus Christ and promote His Gospel through the written word.

We believe through the publication of Christian literature, Jesus Christ and His Word will be exalted, believers will be strengthened in their walk with Him, and the lost will be directed to Jesus Christ as the only way of salvation.

For more information about AMBASSADOR INTERNATIONAL please visit:

www.ambassador-international.com
@AmbassadorIntl
www.facebook.com/AmbassadorIntl

Thank you for reading this book!

You make it possible for us to fulfill our mission, and we are grateful for your partnership.

To help further our mission, please consider leaving us a review on your social media, favorite retailer's website, Goodreads or Bookbub, or our website, and check out some of the books on the following page!

More from Ambassador International

Most of us know Who Jesus is and would admit He was a good and kind Teacher while here on earth. But He is so much more than just a good and kind Teacher—He is our Savior and God and worthy of all our worship. Through an in-depth study into the book of Hebrews, Joshua West and Gary Wilkerson take apart each verse, drawing the reader to a closer look at the Man Who lived here on earth for a short time and then became our Sacrifice to save us from our sins and live with us eternally in Heaven with Him. If you are searching for something more from God, dive into this study and drink in the jaw-dropping beauty of our Jesus.

When our passions overtake us—as they often will—compulsive and addictive behaviors can set in. In *Misguided Passions and the Lord's Prayer*, Curt Richards examines the Lord's Prayer line by line and draws out comforting and reassuring insights that can be applied to the daily lives of anyone, especially those struggling with misguided passions. Richards shines a light on the beautiful universal truths found in the Lord's Prayer.

In a world that is full of chaos and change, many people turn to the Psalms to find comfort in times of stress. In *A Harmony of Two Psalms*, Guy Robert Peel Steward takes a closer look at two of those psalms—Psalm 2 and 91—and analyzes their key truths, hoping to shine some light for the reader on what the words truly mean and how they can find comfort in the God Who sees the chaos and offers rest in the storm. Be challenged in your knowledge of God's Word and learn more about some of the verses that can soothe our weary souls.

www.ingramcontent.com/pod-product-compliance
Lightning Source LLC
Chambersburg PA
CBHW062223080426
42734CB00010B/1998